Post-Tribal Shamanism

A New Look at the Old Ways

Post-Tribal Shamanism

A New Look at the Old Ways

Kenn Day

MOON
BOOKS

Winchester, UK
Washington, USA

First published by Moon Books, 2014
Moon Books is an imprint of John Hunt Publishing Ltd., Laurel House, Station Approach,
Alresford, Hants, SO24 9JH, UK
office1@jhpbooks.net
www.johnhuntpublishing.com
www.moon-books.net

For distributor details and how to order please visit the 'Ordering' section on our website.

Text copyright: Kenn Day 2013

ISBN: 978 1 78099 619 6

A CIP catalogue record for this book is available from the British Library.

Design: Lee Nash
Illustration: Candace Walkup

Printed and bound by CPI Group (UK) Ltd, Croydon, CR0 4YY

We operate a distinctive and ethical publishing philosophy in all
areas of our business, from our global network of authors to
production and worldwide distribution.

CONTENTS

Acknowledgements

I received these teachings from Grandfather – spirit ally, friend and teacher. May his teachings be received with an open heart and awakened soul. If Grandfather has an external reflection, it is my dear friend and mentor, Elisheva Nesher, from whom I have learned much about the tribal nature of us hairless monkeys.

Many thanks to my beloved wife, Patricia, without whom this book might still be just another good idea. I would also like to express my gratitude to my other readers/editors – Elijah Peterson, Mark Jaruzel and Daniel Brown as well as my many students who have helped me to draw out these teachings into their current shape.

Preface

It is difficult to find words to describe clearly the unseen worlds of the shaman and the work the shaman does. Thirty years of practice passing on these teachings in person have allowed me to do a fair dance with this, but putting it into writing is a further challenge. I hope that the essence of the teachings will be transmitted through these pages, much as Grandfather transmits the teachings through my voice in workshops.

It is necessary to address the issue of cultural appropriation. I use the term post-tribal out of respect for all those who came before us, for those cultures which still exist alongside ours and whose survival is threatened by the aggressive character of our own culture. It is important that what we do does not take anything away from these tribal cultures, but that it does add something fundamental to our own understanding of the larger world, which includes the full spectrum of cultural expression. If I were to teach how to be a tribal shaman, or how to be a tribal person, that would be cultural appropriation. I teach instead how the role of the shaman continues, in a different state, within our current social structure. I never pass on teachings that I have received from tribal sources, both out of respect for their heritage and because those teachings are generally less appropriate for our post-tribal culture than they are within the contexts of their own culture.

I switch back and forth between genders when describing both the tribal and the post-tribal shaman, because men and women are equally adept at these roles and deserve equal acknowledgement.

Most readers will not be considering taking on the role of post-tribal shaman. However, just to be clear: no book or workshop can make you into a shaman, even if you have received the call. Becoming a post-tribal shaman requires the talent, the call and the training, from which the necessary skills may be developed. But the tools of the post-tribal shaman can still provide you with life-enriching experience and realizations.

The use of the teachings outlined in these pages has brought me great joy and profound peace. They have led me to where I am in my life now, which is a very good place. I wish you all blessings on your own journeys and may these teachings bring you to a good place as well.

Introduction

Post-tribal shamanism is a term I coined many years ago to describe this set of received shamanic teachings that are specifically directed to those of us who have been born into an age of tribeless wanderers – who no longer have the life-long connections that bind us to places and people like our ancestors.

Modern life is lived cut off from our souls, ancestors, earth and other elements of what once made life worth living. Our souls still yearn for these missing pieces. Post-tribal shamanism offers a means of reclaiming many of these pieces, not by a return to the past, but by moving forward into a deeper understanding of our place in the universe.

We needn't take these teachings as fact. I encourage you to explore and come to your own conclusions. Engaging these practices in a rigorous manner reveals a way of relating to and being in the world that typically leads to these views and offers the various parts of the self an opportunity for healing, awakening and realization.

The teachings I am passing on in these pages came to me in the greater part from a person I call Grandfather. He is a spirit ally who has been with me for most of my life, if not for many lifetimes before. I have communicated with him regularly during the early 1980s, yet he still remains a mystery. The process of following the suggestions he gave me made me realize that they were effective and that led me to validate his existence. Parts of my ego still insist that he is nothing more than a figment of my overly active imagination. However, the teachings have proven themselves to me and others, and they deserve attention on their own merit.

When I use the term 'shaman' in this text, I am generally referring to the role as expressed through the teachings I received from Grandfather. In many ways these are similar to the teachings of traditional shamans; however there are areas where they differ, due to cultural evolution and the situation in which we find ourselves.

According to Mircea Eliade, a renowned anthropologist and acknowledged expert on tribal shamanism, the term šamán comes originally from the Tungus region of Siberia, where it means 'to know.' He goes on to define shamanism in a number of different ways, including 'a technique of ecstasy.' He also suggests that the term shaman be applied to all practitioners of related techniques anywhere in the world. We have come to use the term shaman to refer to healers from Korea to Canada, Australia to the Amazon, even in the United States this way.

The outline of this book roughly follows the content of a series of workshops I call Post-Tribal Shamanic Training. The book is a valuable text for use with the workshops, and I hope it will also be an equally valuable tool for many whom I never meet or teach in person.

Part I:

What is Shamanism?

Chapter I

Definitions and Destinations

The role of the shaman has drifted, along with all other societal roles during the thousands of years of human cultural evolution. Our role today, in the context of post-tribal culture, is narrower than perhaps ever before. The process of specialization has picked away at this role, breaking out into priest, scholar, story-teller, doctor, psychotherapist, and such, until what is left is the task of healing the soul and acting as psychopomp for those who are dying. So it doesn't make a great deal of sense to look to traditional tribal cultures for the whole picture of what a shaman is for us. At the same time, I have yet to meet a traditional 'shaman' with whom I didn't have an experience of mutual recognition, including a Sangoma from South Africa, elders of the Quero from Peru, a BønPo from Tibet, Lakota elders, Cherokee Medicine People, even a Tuvan shaman from near Mongolia. While much is changed, the root remains the same.

This common root is the stance the shaman takes in service to community, acting as a bridge and sometime guardian between the people of the community and the mysteries of the unknown. While how we view the unknown has changed dramatically, this root paradigm has been the determining factor of shamanic practice through all its permutations.

Today, in our culture, the shaman stands between the post-industrial, high tech world of television, computers, cell phones and the equally invisible world of Mystery, Spirit and soul. Unlike the cultures before ours, which placed a high value on these unknowable things, ours barely acknowledges them. So the shaman's position is made more difficult by the belief that we are standing for something that doesn't even exist. The benefits we receive from the post-tribal shaman's work are substantial and profound, connecting us with our root of identity, healing soul wounds that cause addictions and destructive behavior, and a wide spectrum of ailments arising from soul loss or trauma.

Many of us have ideas about the invisible world, but we have been so deeply influenced by the attitudes of our surrounding culture that, even if we think we believe in the invisible and ineffable world of Spirit, it remains only an idea. Only the direct experience of spirit beings can change that deeply rooted opinion, and even then, it often takes many experiences over an extended period of time to really shift things.

This narrow focus of the post-tribal shaman supports deeper movement into the realm of the spirit than that of a traditional shaman, whose roles include more responsibilities for maintaining the physical, emotional and spiritual health of their community. The traditional community views its connections with ancestors, spirits and the earth as a part of everyday life, part of their natural world. Our modern culture has spent so long cutting itself off from these elements of the natural world that we are left adrift, and so our post-tribal shaman's work is often concerned with bringing us back into connection and balance with these very important pieces of the whole which provide a root to our identity and sense of belonging.

In observing traditional shamans, I have found that they often share very little of their own personal journey with those they serve. They already have a whole world in common with the rest of their tribe, including a rich internal world in which they are at one with their ancestors, tribal guardians and the spirits of their land, so their focus is on maintaining the identity and cohesion of the tribe. They keep the individual members of the tribe in good relationship with the ancestors, spirit, earth and the numinous or divine, as experienced by that tribe.

The post-tribal shaman serves people from a wide array of cultures, with very little grounding in their ancestral heritage, encounters a different internal landscape with each new client, which means that some of the focus is on exploring that landscape and, in most cases, helping the client to explore it as well.

The tribal shaman is in service to the tribe as a whole. The health, well-being, strength and survival of that whole take precedence over the needs of any of the individuals within the tribe. Further, the role of the tribal shaman is essentially conservative. He strives to keep things as they are, as they have been for generations. He will only work to help the tribe change if the survival of the whole tribe is threatened. The spiritual health of his charges is addressed by keeping the tribe as a whole on good terms with Spirit. The idea of assisting in the personal spiritual evolution of an individual doesn't appear in his job description.

By contrast, the post-tribal shaman is in service to and necessarily more focused on the process of individual transformation, integration and awakening the soul – both in themselves and in their clients.

These changes are an evolutionary shift in what is needed from the shaman to maintain the health of their charges. In a tribe, the health of the group is maintained by keeping things from changing. In a world in which change is an inescapable reality of everyday life, the health of individuals is supported by helping them to change.

In my own work, an increasing number of clients are seeking support in awakening their soul. I could offer any number of theories, but since I view shamanism as an essentially phenomenological practice, I will try to speak instead about what I observe and the teachings I have received that support these observations.

Most of the teachings are pragmatic and practical. For instance, the human soul needs connection. When it doesn't experience enough connection, it hungers for it. This hunger can cause addictions in the realm of the ego, because it doesn't recognize what the soul is actually yearning for. All it knows is the hunger, which it responds to as best it can. These responses generally take the form of alcoholism, drug addiction and other forms of addictive behavior. By bringing the soul back into connection with ancestors, Spirit, earth and the numinous, addictions tend to diminish until they disappear.

The practice of the post-tribal shaman is paradoxical. It is a dance in which one foot remains in the ordinary world, while the other takes journeys into entirely different realities. It is a way of holding the finite and infinite together within the body and soul. This juggling act is essential to the role of the post-tribal shaman.

My own definition of what a post-tribal shaman is has shifted and changed as the process has shifted and changed me. It began with Mircea Eliade's list of what makes a shaman, then simplified to 'anyone using altered states of consciousness to bring about changes (healing) and retrieve information in ways other than ordinary medicine.' Experience taught me that even this definition was too intellectual and didn't speak to the initiatory depth or the spiritual vitality of the role. The definition I use today is 'anyone who, in service to the healing, growth and awakening of his or her community, stands as a bridge between the known and the unknown.'

Chapter 2

Social Evolution

The role of the shaman is as old as humanity itself. Shamans – both male and female, by all their different names – have long been a respected part of tribal culture, both historically and in contemporary indigenous settings. It may seem that this pivotal role was lost when humans moved away from their hunter-gatherer origins and into cities. This is not so.

While the role of the shaman has become submerged, it is now needed more than ever in our hectic, disconnected life. Most people just don't realize this.

The shaman has always existed in a symbiotic relationship with the community it serves: thus, as that community evolves, so does the shaman. Thus the tribal shamans are not exactly what we need as modern humans, though they can help us find the way to what a post-tribal shaman is today.

In some ways, the need we have for a shaman in our modern world is similar to that of the tribal world. We need the shaman to act as a bridge between the seen and the unseen; to act as a conduit for spirit; to help us to heal the wounds of the soul; and, to help us to move beyond this world with ease, when the time comes to die. In these ways, post-tribal shamans are the same as those tribal shamans who came before us.

In other ways, the need for the shaman is very different from how it is in a tribal setting. The deepest needs that call to the shaman today are the soul's wounds, the invisible wounds that are epidemic in our post-tribal culture. These needs, that literally call the shamans into existence, have a very visible impact on our world. We see the evidence of this wound in the pervasive sense of disconnection and lack of belonging throughout Western culture. We see it in the increasing issues of addiction and self-destructive behaviors. We see it in our own personal lack of connection, with each other, with our world and with ourselves. These issues are a great part of what the post-tribal shaman addresses in her service to community.

To understand these shifts in social evolution and how they impact us today, we need to understand something of the tribal context from which we emerge. To understand traditional shamans and their practice requires a grasp of the world in which they live and work. This world is so fundamentally different from ours as to be beyond comprehension, but I hope to at least give some sense of how far we have come from that place.

Tribal culture varies greatly around the world, and yet there are certain elements that arise consistently throughout. So we can speak of tribal culture, to some degree, as a universal, in that it applies to tribal groups located in all parts of the globe.

In tribal culture, the most important unit is the tribe. The needs, desires and rights of the individual are subservient to the needs, desires and rights of the tribe as a whole. When there is conflict between the tribe and an individual, the tribe takes precedence. Thus the culture of the tribe is essentially conservative, because it seeks to maintain the status quo. This status quo is maintained in a number of ways: continuity of myth, ancestral connection with the land spirits, adherence to social roles and customs, and communal participation in rituals that reaffirm the connections of the tribe to the ancestors, the land, and the tribal identity.

The identity of each tribe is based on its creation and ancestor myths. These myths are learned by children at the knee of their elders, and they are worked into the images and motifs that surround them in their homes, their community space, and in their understanding of the world around them. These stories often describe the emergence of the people of the tribe into this world, from some previous world, through a landmark on their ancestral lands. These stories go on to provide a sense of the relationship the people have with the world around them and their purpose in this world. All of this is quite clear, and all members belong to the tribe through their adherence to their place in the stories. These form the foundation of their sense of identity, both as a tribe and as individuals.

This sense of tribal identity provides a foundation of positive self-esteem and self-regard, based on the sense of belonging that comes with adhering to the structures, rituals, taboos and attitudes of the communal whole. There is no need to ask some of the most stressful questions modern humans encounter, such as: Who am I? Where do I come from? What is my purpose? These questions are already answered, and they look back to the long line of their ancestors, whose success in surviving and passing on life is validation for their answers.

Tribal culture carries with it an inherent assumption of a divide between 'us and them' in much the way as our modern culture assumes a division between 'self and other.' We still see echoes of this attitude in professional sports, elections and wars between nations, but the us and them divide is now much less important than that between our individual self and the rest of the world.

Post-tribal society has come to value the individual above the collective, and this is nowhere so extreme as in the United States, where the Rugged Individualist has become a national icon of all the virtues that we hold dear.

Some years ago, my dear friend and mentor Elisheva was conducting a workshop with me on building community in our post-tribal culture. She asked one question that brought the essence of how different our culture is into focus: 'Imagine you could live anywhere you wanted, but that you would have to live there, with those people, in that place, for the rest of your life. You could travel wherever you wanted to, but this would be the only home you would return to. How does it feel to picture this?' Almost everyone had a negative response, ranging from mild discomfort to agitated rejection of the very idea. This is hardly unique. Those raised in our culture are taught that putting down roots is the next thing to digging your own grave.

Tribal culture is held together by a web of myth, tradition and ceremony, tying the people of the tribe to the land their ancestors lived on and are buried within. By contrast, our modern culture is beset by contradictory myths and symbols, conflicting traditions and empty ceremonies, with little or no connection to the land we live on and only fading memories to honor those who come before us.

The upside of this evolutionary movement is that we also have unprecedented access to information about the nature of the physical world and how it works. New technological breakthroughs occur on an almost daily basis, which will hopefully lead – eventually – to a greater balance, as we come to respect and honor the place we all came from. However, the most significant outcome of this movement is the idea of personal sovereignty. Every individual in our culture has, if only in the abstract, the same rights, privileges and opportunities – as well as an equal sense of standing in the center of his or her universe, acting upon their world. This allows us to move from one side of the globe to the other, to go from poverty to riches in a single lifetime; to reinvent ourselves with astonishing ease, and to live a life in which change is the only constant. In this sense, individuals now wield powers greater than whole nations did only a few hundred years ago.

The values of the traditional culture are based on the need to maintain the balance between available resources and size of the community reliant on the resources. The values of our modern culture stand in contrast to these traditional values, in that they are based on a need to maintain and accentuate the individuation and sovereignty of the self. Since we are no longer tied to the land by our need to work it, we are also free to move anywhere we desire. If the resources of a particular area are depleted, we move on. If we don't like the job we have, the house we live in or the community around us, we move. This capacity was undreamed of by our ancestors.

To put it most succinctly, traditional culture was about keeping things the way they were, in order to maintain the cohesion of the community. Post-tribal culture is focused on the diverse needs of individuals, which only connect temporarily into anything resembling community.

These would not be problems if individuals were truly ready to engage their lives without significant connection to others, but such is not the case. This evolutionary shift has broken down the traditional ties of the soul with family, community, land and spirit, leaving the individual bereft of these profound supports. But we have not evolved beyond the deep need for these connections, and so our souls hunger for something that is no longer understood or readily available. Everything has changed and everything remains the same.

Tribal culture recognizes the call of the shaman and the necessity of training and initiation in the process of the person called becoming a shaman. The tribe values the shaman and acknowledges the sacrifices made in order to walk that path. This sense of recognition, inclusion and respect for the shaman's service provides a much-needed matrix in which the shaman can work most effectively. The person being called to shamanize in our culture often lacks the context, support and understanding with which to respond to such a call, and yet many of us do respond. It is my hope that the teachings of post-tribal shamanism will help to provide a healthy and effective context for generations of shamans yet to come. Yet it needs to be clearly stated that no one part of this process can make someone a shaman. It is not enough to have the call without the training. The training is not sufficient without the initiatory experiences. Even having a spirit ally does not qualify you as a post-tribal shaman. Only when all of these pieces are integrated into a cohesive whole will the post-tribal shaman begin to serve effectively.

Chapter 3

Shamanic Cosmology

There is only one center – it just happens to be everywhere.
  – Grandfather

The post-tribal shaman views the world in much the same way as the tribal shaman. Perhaps the most significant difference between these world views is that the post-tribal shaman needs to deal with many more maps of the same territory. Unlike the tribal shaman, each of our clients comes to us with a different sense of the world and their place in it, as well as their relationship with their ancestors and other important spirits.

Our modern culture has no cohesive mythos; no internal sense of our connections with one another or the land we live on. In some ways, this is a blessing. It allows for a considerable degree of mobility between economic levels and social classes. It makes it easier to leave home, when we choose to attend a college thousands of miles away, or take a job in another country. It makes new connections possible which were hard to image under the old way of viewing the world.

Within tribal culture, we see our own history. We see tribes in which the same souls have incarnated time and time again, strengthening the weave of the fabric of the clan. We see a reverence for the ancestors that maintains their presence within the family, allowing their blessings to have a beneficial impact on their descendants. We see a connection to the land, and to the spirit of the land, strengthened by the bones of the ancestors buried there. We see the relationship between the ordinary and the numinous, from which our own religions arose.

We also see the dark side of our history. We see entangled communities in which there is no room for individuals to manifest their own potential. We see the resistance to change of any kind, simply because change is a danger to how things have always been. We see taboos rigidly followed, even when the reasons for them are long forgotten.

In the cosmology of the tribal shaman, history begins with the entrance of the people of the tribe into this world. Where they come from is outside time and thus outside history. It is a space in which the shaman can travel, but which is impenetrable to the rest of the tribe. Because our culture is made up of many peoples, who emerged into this world in many different ways, we will go back further to set the ground of mythical emergence.

Before the beginning, in a place that is not a place, where time does not yet exist, there is the One. The One is all that IS, and it floats in the Void, which is NOT. The One contains all possibility, including its own extension into the many worlds of manifestation. This begins as the One sees its reflection in the Void, and in startled response, it leaps away from itself. This primordial flight of the One from its reflection creates space, which allows for time, and as the One (which is now two) flees from that first encounter, it begins to slow and to yearn for its Oneness. This yearning causes it to reverse its course, to begin to seek that from which it ran. Keep in mind that both of these two are the One. It is only its confusion that has allowed it to forget itself. As it returns to itself, it rushes toward union, only to discover that it has polarized into matter and energy, dark and light, and can no longer return to its previous state. Instead, as these two parts of the One embrace and seek to merge, they experience one another. Matter experiences energy moving within it – animating it. Energy feels itself contained. Both these experiences are manifestations of the child of these two: Consciousness. And this is how the world is born, grounded in the infinite expansion of the One.

This manifestation contains all the worlds; all the realms; all possibility, because it is the expansion of the One, which is All. It also contains the worlds of the shaman. How could it be otherwise?

Rather than offer a scholarly review of how different cultures around the world have mapped the shamanic realms, I will offer the maps I have drawn for myself from my own explorations. They are substantially similar to the maps of tribal shamans throughout the world. However, for those interested in cross-cultural comparison, I recommend the works of Mircea Eliade and Holger Kalweit.

There are three worlds: the Upper World, Middle World and Lower World and, connected by the World Tree, whose trunk spans all three. These three worlds have much in common, but they are each unique reflections of the whole.

The Middle World is a reflection of this world in which we live. It has everything that is out there in the ordinary universe, but with some important differences. You can, for instance, travel through time as easily as you traverse space. If you want to return to your childhood home, you can. You can go to the house as it is now, or you can journey back to how it was when you were a child. The Middle World is populated by a wide variety of nature spirits, plant spirits, animal spirits and lesser spirits of all types. It is where you would go to meet and develop a relationship with one of these sorts of spirits (more on that in a later chapter).

The Upper World emerges from the higher limbs of the World Tree, but once you are away from the trunk of the tree, it looks much the same as the Middle World, with sky and earth and all. However, it is always less substantial than the Middle World, and considerably less so than the Lower World. Here we find spirits of a more celestial character. Many gods and goddesses can be found here, as well as the spirits of those teachers who no longer want to take on human form in the Middle World, but still want to be of service.

The Lower World can be found beneath the roots of the World

Tree. As you move away from the tree, the Lower World also looks much as you would expect, with sky and earth and everything else. However, it remains much denser than the other worlds and for this, and other reasons, can be the most dangerous of the three worlds. It is dangerous because this greater density can mean greater impact, at every level of our being. It is here in the Lower World that the ancestors dwell, along with the greater animal spirits. It is also a good place to go looking for ways to heal the deepest wounds, because the Lower World is also where we hide some parts of our self that we are unable to acknowledge or recognize within us.

This map would be recognized by tribal shamans around the world. They might draw things differently, but they know the territory it describes. This is the world which contains the ancestors, the spirits of the earth and the divine spirits of the world beyond ours. The map also shows where we come from and where we go after death. When we die, there is a part that remains here. Many cultures have ways of dealing with this part. Grandfather suggests encouraging it to move to a comfortable resting place – a favorite tree or rock – where it can gradually become part of the natural world.

The rest of us leaves this world at the death of the physical body and is welcomed by the ancestors in the Lower World. Here, we have the opportunity to resolve any unfinished business from this life and settle into our role as an ancestor within the larger family soul of all our blood relations. Once a certain level of resolution has been achieved, the celestial part of our soul separates from the ancestor part and rises up the tree into the Upper World. This is the part that has lived many lifetimes and will probably choose to live many more. Depending on how awake this part is, it may be drawn back into a lifetime based upon the experiences of the past lifetimes, it may choose a particular place to incarnate, or it may choose to remain in the Upper World without taking on a physical body.

In tribal culture, the celestial soul is born again and again into the same tribe, but I rarely see this practiced in families not raised in such a culture.

If the celestial soul decides to take on another body, it will be drawn back down the tree to the Middle World, and into the body of a newborn baby with its first breath. Here it joins with the ancestral soul of this body, which connects it with all the ancestors of that bloodline. Together, they will work with the senses of the new body to create a new part, which we generally refer to as the ego. When the physical body dies, this is the part that usually remains behind.

The shamanic perspective on the soul answered several questions for me. It helped me to understand how there could be a part of me that is completely convinced that it will die when my body dies, while another part of me is equally certain that it will continue on. It also showed me how important the process of integration is for shamanic practice. The action of bringing these different pieces together as one, and bringing them to more wakeful states, is essential for the more advanced teachings I've received. These teachings ultimately lead to being able to so integrate all the parts of the self into the awareness of the soul, that you can maintain continuity of consciousness even after death. You can even draw the physical body into this awareness to the point that it ceases to be physical and returns to its energetic nature, disappearing into light. Or so Grandfather tells me. I've not tried it yet, and I'm in no hurry to do so.

These teachings also make it clear that we owe a profound loyalty to our ancestors, because, in a very real sense, we are them. At the same time, a split exists within us between that ancestral soul and the celestial soul, which may have an agenda of its own, and which doesn't align with the ancestral soul. These phenomena can lead to entanglements at a deeper level than most psychotherapies can reach. Such confusions are uncommon in tribal settings, because their infinite and ancestral souls are used to working in tandem. So, issues of cultural appropriation aside, we cannot borrow techniques from tribal shamans, but have to address these new issues ourselves, with the aid of our spirit allies and teachers.

Culture is a reflection of myth, and myth is a reflection of culture. Like the One mistaking its reflection for Other, culture and myth rarely recognize the nature of their relationship. They are two manifestations of One.

The culture of the tribe is essentially conservative; it seeks to keep things as they were for the ancestors, so that the children born to the tribe will have as much as the parents did. This is the antitheses of the culture of modern America, where it is assumed that each generation has the opportunity to provide more for the next generation than what it grew up with; it is a culture where just doing as well as your parents did is viewed as failure. No wonder that we have such problems with materialism, addiction and stress. We are no longer connected with those things which most feed our souls. Instead we have replaced them with disconnected yearnings, with unquenchable thirst and distorted hungers. Materialism has replaced spirituality.

Fortunately for our post-tribal culture, and for us as individuals, this is not the end of the story. We have ample opportunity to reconnect with what feeds our souls, and in doing so, to heal the invisible wounds that have plagued us for so long. I will go into some of the practices we can use to heal these wounds on an individual level later in this book, but the short answer is: find those things for which your soul hungers and hold them close: reconnect with your ancestors, the earth, Spirit – with all the things your soul holds dear.

Chapter 4

The Role of the Shaman

We can define what we mean by the term post-tribal shaman in our culture in many ways, but basically it is not all that different from how we define the term 'doctor.' A person can go to medical school and earn his or her medical degree, but until they go into practice, they are rarely referred to as a doctor. In the same way, a shaman is not simply someone who has the training, or even the Call. It is someone who has both the training and the call AND has put their skills to use in service to their community.

What this service looks like will differ from person to person. Each shaman has different skills, is aligned with different spirit allies and draws on different teachings. In addition, each client offers different challenges and may call for different perspectives.

Certainly the range of roles of the shaman in contemporary culture is much diminished from that played in a tribal setting. Perhaps it began rather simply, as the one who stood between the community and the unknown, in service to his or her tribe. This primal role is the basis of everything from priest and prophet to judge and storyteller.

Most of the jobs arising from the primal stance of the tribal shaman have been taken up by others, through the process of specialization. At the same time, the form of the unknown has also shifted and shrunk, as science has come to explain many of the mysteries of the past. What is left is a more specific role in dealing with a narrower, but very deep, unknown: the realm of Spirit.

In our current culture, Spirit is both unknown and overly defined. There are an almost infinite number of books claiming to clarify the vagaries of the afterlife, faerie or power animals.

But most of these books only add to the confusion, because they treat Spirit as an intellectual exercise, which can be approached, contained and explained by the mind alone. The perspective I suggest is somewhat different: while intellectual investigations of Spirit may be partly satisfying for our mind, Spirit is real in a way that is deeper than abstract, mental notions. It is real in the way that stones are real, that water is real. It is a part of the natural world, just as we are. But for most of us, practices are needed such as those that will be described in subsequent chapters for us to be able to experience Spirit in these ways.

The role that the shaman fills in our culture is strangely practical. I say strangely, because our views of Spirit lead one to expect those who work in that area to be ungrounded in the ordinary realities of life. Nothing could be further from the truth. The post-tribal shaman must be more grounded than anyone, since, while he or she extends into the spirit realm, they must remain rooted here, both for themselves and for their clients. A shaman who gets lost when traveling in the shamanic realms is of no use to anyone.

We can define the role of post-tribal shaman in any number of ways, but it still comes down to standing between the unknown and the community – their clients. The role the shaman plays in his or her community depends on the needs of their clients as well as the shaman's own talents and connections with spirits, but the shape of that role is pretty consistent. Whether the client needs intercession with ancestors or with their own body, they come to address issues that are not being dealt with elsewhere.

How does someone in our culture experience the shaman today? Most only interact with a shaman through a professional relationship, in which they visit the shaman's office for sessions. I am one of these professional shamans, who work out of an office and charge an hourly rate, so I can speak to a great extent on what role the shaman plays in this setting.

More rarely, the shaman acts as a leader in community ritual, rites of passage and ceremonies. Several times a year, I am asked to officiate at weddings. Occasionally I perform funerals. I also design and lead celebratory ceremonies and transformative rituals at various festivals and conferences. I even perform house blessings and exorcisms. All of these fall under the job description of the post-tribal shaman, as do various other functions not listed here.

The less apparent, but equally important role of the shaman is to act as a provocateur, and instigator of awakening and realization, which generally occurs without any overt action on the part of the practitioner. Performing the practices, developing and maintaining the connections with Spirit: all change the resonance of the individual. This process resonates with others to stir those parts of the soul that are ready to emerge and bring them to the surface where they can blossom into awareness.

Chapter 5

A Link with Our Ancestors

Humans have lived here on earth for at least the past 200,000 years in some form. During this time, we have evolved a way of engaging with each other and the world around us that was substantially the same for the greater part of that time. It is only in the past few hundred years that our cultures have evolved in directions that radically alter the relationships that have been essential to the foundation of the human experience for so long.

At a soul level, the longstanding links between ourselves and our ancestors still remain. It is the ego which no longer experiences the sense of connection, support and blessing that flows from the generations that came before us. Yet my own experience working as a shaman in our post-tribal culture is that even the ego senses that something is missing and feels bereft.

As a post-tribal shaman, one of my most important jobs is helping others to reconnect with their ancestors, bringing them into alignment with the communal ancestral soul.

The root of this linkage, what makes it so essential to us even today, is that we evolved from a more communal state of consciousness. I doubt that humans were ever quite as integrated as a hive of bees or a nest of ants, but the indications of a communal soul are present even in the traditional cultures that still exist today. If you speak with an elder of a tribal culture, you will see that they identify more strongly with their tribe as a whole than with themselves as individuals. Most tribal cultures support this paradigm through how the children in the tribe are raised. They are taught that the tribe comes first; that the ancestors are an important part of their daily lives; that the spirits require respect; and that they have a place in the world as a people. Their individual identity is rooted in this strong sense of tribal identity. They know who they are as individuals because they know who they are as a tribe. Consider how this contrasts with today's focus on the individual. You would never see a youth growing up in such a culture needing to 'find himself.'

It is important to note that, without a clear spiritual connection between our ancestors and our ego, we are like collarless dogs. We don't really know where we belong, and that makes it almost impossible to know real peace and joy. We may supplement the ancestral lineage with spiritual or emotional connections, but these cannot and do not effectively take the place of those who gave us life.

The awareness of the communal ancestral soul is one of our most powerful means of sensing how we belong within this world. Being able to allow the individual self to take refuge in the greater soul of the family or the tribe is powerfully healing in ways that are sadly incomprehensible to most modern individuals.

Because so much of the post-tribal shaman's work is focused on developing and maintaining a healthy link between his or herself and their ancestors, or between the client and their ancestors, we have developed many ways to accomplish this. In the second part of this book, you will learn practices which develop and strengthen your ancestral ties, bringing greater abundance, blessings and a profound sense of belonging.

Chapter 6

Post-Tribal Shamanic Ethics

The work of a post-tribal shaman takes both shaman and client beyond the boundaries of the ordinary world in which we live our everyday lives. The journey of healing is often challenging, frightening and incomprehensible. In order to embark on this journey, the shaman must know the landscape they will encounter and the spirits who inhabit it, but most of all he must know himself. The shaman is to act as a guide as well as healer, and he, or she, needs to be worthy of the client's trust. In order to earn this trust, he must know that he will not act in ways that are harmful to the client. He must have clear boundaries within which he knows he will operate. These boundaries are the professional ethics of the post-tribal shaman's practice – the values and standards by which the shaman conducts himself, or herself.

There is no professional association of shamans, no universal code which all choose to follow, and so ethics will vary somewhat from one practitioner to another. The root of these values is not unlike the Hippocratic Oath medical doctors follow: first, do no harm. The post-tribal shaman seeks to do no harm as well, but is also guided by a need to help clients to transform themselves. The means by which this transformation is achieved lie beyond the expectations of the client, and often of the shaman as well. The means may include taking the client on shamanic journeys into other worlds, conversing with the ancestors or other spirits, reconnecting parts of the soul, and various other inexplicable actions.

The practice of shamanism falls outside any license, so it is up to each individual practitioner to set his or her own boundaries, based on his or her own values and experience. While we are not doctors or psychotherapists, their ethics are not a bad place to

26

start. I've borrowed some of my own professional ethics from these established sources.

- Do no harm;
- Respect your client;
- Don't take advantage of your client;
- Don't sleep with your client;
- Maintain confidentiality; and,
- Don't take on a client who you know you can't help.

Beyond these basic parameters things get more challenging.

Transformation and awakening are often distinctly uncomfortable processes, so it is unproductive to use the client's comfort level as a reliable gauge. At the same time, it must be remembered that, unlike many forms of therapy practiced today, the post-tribal shaman knows herself to be in service to the client, and so the client is ultimately the one in charge of the process. What I mean by being in service is that, rather than the post-tribal shaman assuming a role of authority relative to the client, he assumes a role of receptive readiness, awaiting the opportunity to provide support or challenge, as required by the process. This needs to be clearly communicated, so that the client is empowered to set his or her own boundaries as well. The paradigm of post-tribal shamanism is working with the client rather than working on the client – while trusting in the process of healing.

One of the elements that sets post-tribal shamanism apart from other therapies is the focus on treating soul wounds. It takes specialized training to develop the set of skills to be able to work at this level, but this alone is not sufficient. We often speak of the shaman being called to this work. This call may appear as a traumatic ordeal, or series of ordeals, which sets the individual apart and sensitizes him to the invisible world. Without these initiatory experiences, studying shamanism is a little like attending art school with no talent. You can take the classes and it will help your understanding and appreciation of art, but you may never be able to create the kind of art you would like to. The post-tribal shaman needs to have the call, the training AND the initiations in order to practice competently.

Too many examples exist of well-intentioned people practicing under the name shaman, with little more than the desire to do so. Under the best circumstances, these 'shamans' offer little more than placebos to their clients. All too often, the circumstances are less than good and the outcome is tragic. Within the past few years alone, a so-called shaman tried to hide the body of a young man who died while undergoing a session with him; in another situation, three clients died in a miss-managed sweat lodge. These are the most extreme and well known examples; many other examples of clients being harmed by poorly trained, uninitiated or unskilled 'shamans' have been brought to light.

The post-tribal shaman is set apart from other healing modalities not only by this focus on soul-level work, but also by the need to work in the realm of the irrational, inexplicable and invisible. Thus the necessary boundaries are difficult to set, because the area the shaman is placing them in is not visible in the usual sense.

The soul is present throughout all parts of our being. It is in our bodies and our minds. In a sense, it is the foundation from which all our other parts arise. When we go looking for soul-level wounds, they may appear anywhere within the spectrum of our life experience. Because soul wounds usually arise from trauma, the process of addressing them and moving toward healing is usually painful and often frightening. Some of these places may be uncomfortable for both the client and the shaman, wounds in the area of the client's sexuality, for example. Here the boundaries need to be very clearly drawn and expressed, so that both parties can feel safe working in difficult territory. To be more specific, no sex with clients – ever. The post-tribal shaman does work with sexual issues, because there are often soul-level wounds in these areas, but they do so in a way that maintains these boundaries. As in psychotherapy, the client may experience intense emotional projections onto the practitioner, if strong desires are being brought up with no clear channel or if there appears to be a confusing soul-level connection with the client. In such cases, if it appears the work cannot be done safely, it is best to refer the client to another therapist.

This work with the soul is best accomplished with help from spirits, who are by their nature more competent in the realm of spirit. Part of the training of the shaman often involves developing a good working relationship with a helping spirit who we refer to as a spirit ally. This ally assists in all phases of the healing, supporting and sometimes amplifying the work of the shaman. The bond between shaman and ally can be quite strong and deep and it may be tempting to follow the spirit's lead without question, but it is important to always consider the consequences to both the client and yourself before doing so. We are not obligated to work with all clients or all wounds. Some are best left to others. It is important for the shaman not to need the client, so that he can walk away when necessary, allowing him to work only in the territory where he is competent. If this cannot be done effectively, the territory needs to be avoided.

The spirits rarely take into account the needs and values of the person's ordinary life, and sometimes the physical body or the ego will pay the price. The shaman has important questions to ask: Is this action appropriate? Will it harm? Is now the time for it? Is it helpful? Is it necessary? It will also be necessary to know which heads the agenda ahead of time – the needs of the client, the spirit allies or the shaman? In general, the client's boundaries must be respected first, but it is also important to respect your own. If the movement suggested by Spirit is beyond your own boundaries, then this needs to be curtailed. If you allow the needs of the client to cross your own boundaries, you will be wounded by it. The shaman needs to know that, though the client is in charge of where the process goes, it is completely appropriate to stop a session if necessary. It is best to refer a client to someone else rather than risk deeper wounding to either party.

A simple example of this in my own practice occurred many years ago, with a client who was regularly pushing my boundaries. She would show up late for appointments and want me to give her extra time at the end of the appointment. She would ask me to do little favors for her on my own time. Essentially she was asking for undue consideration, beyond what I offered to my other clients. I began to feel resentful and frustrated and eventually blew-up at her at the end of yet another session in which she felt I should extend her time. This was unprofessional of me, but the cause of it was granting too many boundary crossings, without even noticing.

Your own soul-level wounds give you blind spots and Shadows which are potentially dangerous to you and your clients. It is part of the responsibility of a post-tribal shaman to actively address your own wounds, engaging in regular spiritual healing and deepening awareness, so that your blind spots are well charted with red flags to warn you of danger areas.

The nature of shamanic work is such that it is easy to wander off in directions that are potentially dangerous. The role of ethics in this work is to provide a set of healthy guidelines that keep us on the path toward healing and integration. This is true both for the personal work one does in their own healing and growth as well as for those who are called to work with others. If you don't learn how to keep on the path with your own work, you can't expect yourself to do so for others.

When I speak with other shamans – either post-tribal or from tribal traditions – they all acknowledge the need to stay connected with the spirits, their own soul, their ancestors and their communities. While the details of how they do this may differ – from person to person and from culture to culture – we share a common root sense of what our responsibilities are toward those we serve. This shared root is the knowledge that we must act with integrity toward our clients.

This is the ground from which the post-tribal shaman's code of ethics arises. What nurtures this ground is the awareness of self and the interconnections with others. When there is a clear understanding of these things, the values become more apparent; it is an on-going process of self-exploration.

One of the most important areas to explore is the nature of the relationship between ego and soul. By ego, I refer to the part of the self that directly experiences this world through the physical senses and, at least until it becomes more aware, thinks of itself as the whole identity. By soul, I refer to the parts of the self that exist before the emergence of ego and after the death of ego. Both soul and ego need to be fully engaged, with mutual respect and with clarity about what areas each is responsible for. The strength of this internal relationship will positively impact the post-tribal shaman's relationships with clients, as well as those with their spirit allies.

The post-tribal shaman explores deeply into the world of spirit, which naturally opens her ego to an ever deepening awareness of soul. As this awareness grows, ego experiences initiations that reshape it to be more and more like that soul. This process allows many of the distortions of ego to drop away. However, the shaman still lives in both worlds. She is both soul and ego, and this paradoxical relationship of self and Self, must be mastered in order to be effective in this work.

Many shamans are tempted to surrender entirely to soul, allowing the dictates of soul to lead all of their movements through life. This may be an appropriate choice for a mystic, but I would argue that it is antithetical to the nature of the shaman. The shaman walks in both worlds, and must learn to navigate effectively and function competently in both. He must also be able to recognize when necessary choices arise and make them, even when it is uncomfortable.

The shamanic experience is paradoxical. The shaman is at once grounded in the everyday life of an ordinary person, while also being held in the awareness of a limitless soul. He is both finite and infinite. He remains conscious of his physical body, even while journeying into other worlds in the shamanic body. The ambiguous nature of shamanic work is in its essence. It is inescapable, and it must be dealt with. The shaman will be exploring unknown territory and will have to make judgment calls on what the best response to situations are as they arise. Inevitably, not all of these judgments will be correct or even ethically appropriate, at least in hindsight. While it is important always to try to come up with the best response in each situation, it is equally important to recognize your limitations and have compassion for your own shortcomings – and to learn from them.

The soul is infinitely wise, but the ego doesn't live in the infinite. It dwells in the very finite world of ordinary life, and if the shaman forgets this, he can wander off the path to the detriment of himself and anyone following him. This can happen when the soul calls for an action that goes outside of the ethical, moral boundaries or integrity of the ego, which can be culturally dependent.

Working with spirit, with one's own ancestral and celestial soul, is intoxicating, seductive and can be dangerous to the health of one's ego. When journeying into the three worlds and conversing with powerful spirits, who seem to have your best interests at heart, it is sometimes difficult to remember to maintain a degree of skepticism. I am speaking now, not of those spirits who would willingly and intentionally deceive you, but of those whose agenda is simply more important to them than your health and well-being. Spirits don't have to play by the rules of this world, but we do.

This is one reason why it is necessary to spend considerable time developing a relationship with any spirit ally. Just as with a human friend, placing such reliance on them means that you need to trust them, and this trust should have a strong basis in experience. Just as you wouldn't necessarily trust someone who you had just met at the market with the keys to your house, you will need to be careful not to give complete trust to any spirit that happens by.

It is this ambiguous state of the post-tribal shaman – needing to listen and engage deeply with Spirit and to open to her own soul, while remaining grounded in the pragmatic considerations of everyday life – that is so challenging to those who walk this path in an authentic way. The tendency is often to err on the side of Spirit; to give more weight to the healing movement suggested by an ally or by soul. The problem is that the client's ego is not necessarily ready or capable of receiving the movement and may reject it violently. Even when the ego is open and accepting, you can move no faster than the soul.

Another challenge of this work is that, with each session, the post-tribal shaman is stepping off into the unknown. She needs to be willing to let go of what she knows to make room for what can be revealed or realized through the process. This requires not only a sensitivity and openness to the flow of Spirit, but also the ability to keep an eye on all the other parts of the whole – the body, mind, ego, breath, energy of both shaman and client – that may respond in a way that requires attention.

There are times in which it is appropriate and effective to push firmly into the client's resistance, in spite of their obvious discomfort, in order to help them come to a healthier and more whole place. However, if they ask to stop; to back off; that must be respected. It doesn't matter if soul is telling you that they could be stuck here for the rest of their life if they don't take advantage of this opportunity. They are in charge of the process. They need to know this and to know that they can trust you to accept this, even if you don't think it is for the best. This respect

33

for the client and for the practitioner's ego are clear examples of what differentiates post-tribal from tribal shamanic practice.

When the shaman engages with a client, it is important for them both to realize that he is in service to the client, not the other way around. The bottom line is to always work and live with integrity. This may look different from one person to the next, from one client to the next. We are all learning and growing and awakening. In most cases, only we know when we have broken with integrity. It is up to us to keep ourselves clear and clean. It is this core sense of integrity that clients perceive and which allows them to trust the shaman to such great depths. There is no shortcut to this. It requires rigorous self-exploration and healing, regular spiritual practice, willingness to confront and engage one's Shadows, and to learn from each mistake.

What can happen when you don't maintain your own practice is clearly illustrated by something I experienced several years ago at an alternative spirituality conference. There was a fellow there who was obviously suffering from some traumatic soul-level wounding. He sought help from one of the people there who was offering shamanic work. The shaman worked with him for a few hours, culminating in bringing him out to the public bonfire, wearing nothing but a bearskin and aggressively pushed him into drawing up the toxic substance of his wounds, reliving memories of his childhood abuse. I was at the fire when they came and I left because I was so uncomfortable with what was happening, but didn't want to make matters worse by adding another layer of confrontation. It seemed to me that the shaman was acting outside of his own capacity. I didn't know the actual circumstances until later, when the client came to me for help. The client was left reeling from the work, ungrounded and re-traumatized. When he went to the shaman who got him into this mess to ask for help, he was told that it wasn't his job to do anything beyond what he had already done. This is unconscionable behavior. You don't open someone up and pull their guts out and then just leave them hanging. If you don't know that you will be around to help them bring it back together, you don't take it apart.

Perhaps the greatest danger to our personal integrity is power. The practice of shamanism can produce significant changes, which is easily perceived as power, but nowhere are we more dangerously powerful than in the eyes of our clients. Their view may be more projection than perception, but it can be just as corrupting. This is why it is so essential to know yourself deeply – to know your hungers and how you respond to them. When you have this knowledge you can carry the power to stir the souls of others awake with relative grace and safety.

Finally, though our community is made up of those who come to us for our help, we need to be aware that there are those who we cannot help. The most apparent are those with illnesses or injuries which are beyond our scope of practice, but it can also include those who are simply a bad fit, who are in our blind spots or who raise red flags for any reason. It is appropriate to have a list of medical professionals whom you trust to offer as referrals.

Part II:

Techniques for a Post-Tribal Shaman

Chapter 7

Journeying in the Shamanic Body

My first experiences with shamanic practice were with a teacher whose technique for journeying consisted of telling us to imagine a hole in the ground and, when the drumming started, to imagine going down the hole. I found the exercise – and the rest of the workshop – very unsatisfying, but assumed that the fault was mine. After all, many others in the workshop received vivid visuals and what seemed like meaningful experiences.

A few years later, I had the opportunity to observe a traditional shaman go journeying. I assumed that his technique would be substantially similar to what I had learned in the workshop, and at first this seemed to be true. He began drumming and his head rocked forward and back, his eyes rolling closed. As I observed him closely I felt myself being drawn into an altered state of consciousness. It became difficult to focus on him, and it seemed as if he were being turned inside-out and then dropped into a deep well. I found myself becoming disoriented and slightly nauseous and I remained like this until he began to drum more rapidly and then stopped, his eyes popping open. This experience was distinctly different from anything I had encountered before. When I questioned him about his way of journeying, explaining my own introduction, he seemed confused. When I demonstrated, asking him to drum for me and heading down my imagined hole in the ground, he laughed, 'That's not journeying. You are not going anywhere outside of this!' He said, tapping my forehead.

I don't remember the fellow's name, or what tribe he belonged to or even where we were. It's only been recently that I remembered the encounter at all. It was around that time that I started listening to Grandfather as he taught me how to move from my physical body into the shamanic body.

These teachings form the foundation of the first workshop in my Post-Tribal Shamanic Training series: Opening Inner Doorways. The 'inner doorways' it refers to are those that stand between the ordinary world and what we will be calling the 'shamanic realms.'

The way that shamanic journeying is generally taught and discussed in the modern world makes it difficult to discern any difference between journeying and creative visualization. Perhaps this is because, not having been raised in a traditional culture, in which the spirit realms are acknowledged and respected, we tend to assume unconsciously that journeying is only in the imagination.

It is one thing to hold an idea in your mind, choosing to believe or not believe. It is quite another to actually experience the foundation of that idea directly. This is equally true for the difference between shamanic journeying and creative visualization, as I show my students in the Opening Inner Doorways workshop. Before doing any journey work, I ask the students to close their eyes and visualize a tree. It can be as tall, powerful and deeply rooted as they can imagine. Then I ask them to shift the tree six feet to their left. This is generally not a problem for them. Later, when they have entered Lodge and met the World Tree, I ask them to try to shift THAT to one side. The response is unanimous that it can't be done. This, I tell them, is the difference between shamanic journeying and creative visualization. While visualization is a powerful and important tool, it is still in the head. Journeying goes beyond this in some mysterious way, allowing us to enter into worlds in which we can bring about real and lasting changes. Journeying is real.

The same holds true at a larger scale for all of these teachings as a whole. It is not enough to understand them on an intellectual level. They only come to life and begin to have a profound impact when they are directly experienced. I encourage you not to accept my words without exploring them yourself. Delve into these depths and find what is there for you.

The teachings I received from Grandfather address the gap between perception and experience and allow for a more dynamic and substantial experience of journeying in the three worlds, while also making the adventure much safer. Only you can judge whether these techniques will be effective for you.

The foundation of the technique is based upon these teachings.

The body we inhabit when journeying in the shamanic worlds is distinct from our physical body. We will refer to it as the 'shamanic body.'

A doorway at your center allows you to move your awareness from the external world to the inner world. You can move your awareness through this doorway and into other worlds that you access through this inner doorway.

A further doorway, which can be accessed from the inner world, leads from the physical into the shamanic world. Once in the shamanic world, you can move about in the Middle World, Upper World or Lower World in your shamanic body.

The technique seems complex at first, but with practice it becomes a matter of reflex, until it can be accomplished without thought.

Begin by moving into your center. The more you can let go of your thoughts and focus your attention on this center, the better. This kind of focus takes practice. So perhaps the first step is to simply practice focusing your awareness on a single point in your heart center and releasing all thoughts that arise.

Once you are able to focus clearly, you can begin opening your senses to the doorway that lies at the depths of this center.

When you can feel the spark of radiant energy emerging from this doorway, you can begin to practice moving through the doorway, to the inner world. This is the first of the inner doorways you will need to pass through, moving from the Outer

World to the Inner. Once you have passed through this doorway and accustomed yourself to being present in the Inner World, you will use the radiant energy emerging from the doorway to create a large mirror, in which you can see – or sense – your reflection. Once you are able to perceive your reflection, create a beam of light running from your heart center, where the doorway sits, through the mirror and on into the heart center of your reflected image. When done properly, you can feel the beam of light as an energetic cord that you plug into the heart center of your reflection, establishing a palpable link between your inner physical body and your inner shamanic body.

Once this link is established, you can enter the beam, move along it as if you were traveling down a tunnel of light, going through the mirror and into your inner shamanic body, through the heart center and out, into your outer shamanic body. As you emerge in your shamanic body, you find yourself sitting in a place I call Lodge. It is an enclosed space directly around the World Tree. It is safe to move into and out of, without worrying about picking up anything nasty from the other realms. Why this is, I really don't know, but Grandfather tells me that it is, and in more than thirty years of practice, I've never encountered anything that leads me to believe otherwise.

The Lodge is a large circular room, surrounded by a dome-like wall. At the center of the space is the trunk of a living tree – the World Tree. This tree connects the Upper and Lower Worlds with the Middle World. It also allows us to travel – in the shamanic body – between these worlds.

Your shamanic body is the vehicle of your shamanic consciousness, much as your physical body is the vehicle for your ordinary state of consciousness. This is the body in which you will learn to move between these worlds, encountering ancestors and other spirits, learning how to retrieve lost parts of yourself and reintegrating them into a more whole and healthy you.

Emerging into your shamanic body in Lodge can be disconcerting to some, so I want to go over the process and what you can expect in some detail. First, it is important to let go of any expectations you might have concerning your perceptions in Lodge, and beyond in the three worlds. The Shamanic Realm is not the world you are used to, and it does not respond in the same way.

Perhaps most importantly, you need to let go of any expectation that you are going to see clearly, as if in a dream, and that what you see will correspond with what others see in the same space. Consensus reality is not nearly as well established in the Shamanic World, so while we can usually agree here in the ordinary world on things like the color red, or what water feels like, over there it can be quite different from one person to another. For instance, when encountering the World Tree, some see it as a huge oak, while others sense a rising column of brilliant energy and still others feel a thick pole of unknown substance. Each person is finding a way to make sense of what they are encountering, putting it into terms that they can understand. These terms differ from one person to the next, but what remains the same is the strong sense that there is SOMETHING there that spans between floor and ceiling. All agree that calling it a 'tree' makes as much sense as anything else, and so we do.

Keep your attention focused on the sensations of being in this new and different body. Be aware of how you feel your weight on the packed earth of the floor. Rub your hands together and feel the skin of each hand encountering the other. Gently explore the skin of your face, your hair, your neck. Practice clenching and relaxing your hands to feel this sensation as well. Make a fist in your physical body. Notice the sensations of stretched skin, pressure of knuckles or fingernails against your palm. Then relax your physical body and do the same thing in your shamanic body, paying attention to how the sensations are similar to those of the physical experience. When you feel ready, try standing up. Feel your weight balanced over your feet. Practice standing and sitting a few times and see how that feels.

You may have noticed your image, when you first sensed it in the mirror. Now you have an opportunity to explore what this body feels like, what it is wearing, how it compares and contrasts with your physical form. Take care to stay inside your shamanic body. It is very tempting to step outside of it and observe it, but in doing so, you lose your connection and drop into a mental awareness, much like visualization.

Gradually you will become more comfortable and your body will begin to take on more substance. Now you are ready to take the next step. If you are attending the workshop series, this will already be included in the training, but you can attempt it on your own as well.

Approach the Tree. Place your palms against it. Rest your forehead against it. Feel its presence; its substance and solidity. Ask for the Tree to grant you the substance and guidance you need to proceed with your work here. Be sure to ask from a place of humility and gratitude, honoring the Tree and its Mystery. You may want to ask the spirit of the Lodge, the one I call Grandfather, to help with this. If he answers, he will appear and reach into the Tree, drawing out some of the substance of the Tree and shaping it into a cord that he ties off inside your body, around your spine, just above your sacrum, so that it emerges from your navel. You now have a cord tying you to the World Tree. You can use this cord to draw sustenance and substance from the Tree, building up the stability and solidity of this shamanic body. This cord will also come in very handy as you begin your journeys beyond the Lodge, since it remains in connection with the Tree, no matter where you may journey. If you get lost or disoriented, all you have to do is tune into the cord, give it a good yank and it will draw you back into Lodge.

This cord is probably your first shamanic tool. There will be others to follow, but none will be more essential to your practice of journeying. Be sure to focus in on it when you enter Lodge. It is important to be able to feel and use your connection with the World Tree. This will become clearer as we continue.

Your first journey will be into the Middle World. The Middle World is much like the world we move around in every day. It has ground and sky, sun and clouds and buildings and people and looks much like the world you are used to.

By now, you have had the opportunity to familiarize yourself with the inside of the Lodge. You know that the trunk of the World Tree rises through the middle of this space, which is contained by a circular wall that curves gently inward as it rises, forming a dome. Your first journey will take you through this wall and into the world beyond, but you need to set your physical preparations first.

This is a good place to mention drumming. Drumming is an excellent means of moving into an altered state of consciousness and it is written about exhaustively in many other places, so all I need to say is that drumming is one of many means of altering your consciousness. That said, there are many other means of going into the necessary state of consciousness so that you can journey. The drum is neither necessary nor is it the best choice for every situation. With practice, you will be able to drum and journey at the same time. When you are just beginning, trying to drum with your physical body, while the rest of you is in Lodge can be more distracting than helpful. It is better to use simple concentration to bring yourself into the state where you can journey. If you feel attached to the idea of journeying with a drum, you can use a recording.

It is tempting to lie down and relax while you are journeying, but I recommend strongly that you sit instead. It is too easy to fall asleep when journeying if you are lying down. Falling asleep on your journey causes you to lose all the substance you have built up in your shamanic body to that point. You can retrieve it later, but better to not lose it in the first place. The best posture for journeying is the same as it is for meditation. You want your spine erect and your buttocks a little off the floor so that your hips are slightly higher than your knees. This takes the strain off your lower back, avoiding the need to adjust your posture.

It is also helpful to journey only for as long as necessary. Often this is no longer than 15 minutes for a single journey. The sitting posture is thus effective and usable for most people.

Follow the directions above to enter Lodge and check in with the Tree. Make sure that you feel substantial and coherent in your shamanic body. You may want to practice some kinesthetic exercises to cultivate your shamanic body, such as rubbing your hands together or stomping your feet, as long as you feel some sensation in your shamanic body.

When you feel that you are ready to begin your journey, go to the wall of the Lodge, in the direction you intuitively feel you want to journey. Run your fingers over the wall. Many experience this wall as being constructed of stretched hides and thick tree boughs. Point your finger into the wall a little above head height and draw a line down the wall. Continue this drawing to create the outline of a door. When the outline is complete, a door will appear.

Step through the door and into the Middle World. Keep in mind that whatever you are experiencing is only your brain's attempt to make sense of something happening beyond the range of its sensors. Once your shamanic body becomes more substantial, you will begin to develop perceptions based on the sensory apparatus of that body.

Once outside the Lodge, you can begin by exploring the immediate area. Walk all the way around the Lodge. See if you can sense anything around you in the distance. Eventually a landscape will begin to take shape, even if it is one you sense through touch and smell. Your awareness will begin to expand into the area around the Lodge and you can begin to explore.

With practice, you will be able to find your way through an expansive landscape that will keep you busy for many journeys to come. There are other ways to explore the Middle World, though. Once you have become comfortable with these journeys beyond the Lodge, you can try this variation.

Think of a place that you want to journey to. It should be a place that you have visited in your physical body and are familiar with. Your visit will be in the present as well. Avoid moving into the past for now. Go to the wall of the Lodge in the direction of your destination. Now think of a door that opens in or near the place that you want to journey to. If it is a natural setting with no doors, you can use a large rock, tree or even the earth. Align the wall of the Lodge with the target door. Place your palms against the wall and will the other side to become the opening at your destination. Run your fingers along the wall, feeling the door take shape beneath them. When you are done, the door is ready. This side of the door is in the Lodge. The other side opens into the space you wish to visit. Open the door and step through. Make sure to leave the door open until you return. Once you are back in Lodge, release the door from the wall of the Lodge. This is an excellent means of journeying to specific places and will be an invaluable technique as you continue your explorations, so it's a good one to practice.

The Middle World reflects much of the world as you know it from your ordinary life. You can visit places in your shamanic body, much as you would in your physical body. With practice, you can even learn to travel to places that you have not been to in the physical world.

Your journeys are not confined to the Middle World, though this is where you will be doing a lot of your personal work, because most of the experiences that impact you in this life have happened in the Middle World; this is where they need to be resolved. You could do enough work in the Middle World to come to a relatively integrated and stable place, with no need to go further. So why would you want to explore beyond, into the Upper and Lower Worlds?

If the Middle World reflects the nature of ordinary life and the ego and of all our experiences of life in this time and place, the Upper World is a reflection of the experiences of our celestial soul and the aspirations of that part of our greater Self. Likewise the Lower World reflects our ancestral soul and some of the more mysterious aspects of human experience. The Lower World is also home to the greater animal and plant spirits, while the Upper World is where you will find those entities who have chosen not to take on human (or other) form at this time, but still wish to pass on their wisdom and teachings. These are the spirits who we refer to as spirit guides, spirit allies or helping spirits and sometimes spirit mentors or teachers. These are spirits who pass along specific teachings for our use. Grandfather is certainly one of these, though he tends to hang out in the Lodge and in the Lower World as well.

The World Tree is a very safe and stable way to journey between these worlds. Once you have mastered the technique, it is also very easy.

Approach the Tree and tune into your cord. Feel the substance of the cord connecting you with the Tree. Relax your mind and allow yourself to feel the Tree, the cord and yourself, all of the same substance. Feel the unifying energy flowing through your shamanic body, the cord and the Tree. As you move deeper into this awareness, you will notice that you can affect the substance of the Tree in somewhat the same way that you can affect the substance of your own body. Begin by drawing some of the Tree substance out, as if you were pulling taffy. With practice, you will be able to use the Tree as a source of energy from which to make and accomplish all manner of things. As you may have already guessed, this is also how your cord was made.

It is quite important to realize that this is not an exercise of the mind. What you are experiencing in Lodge and in the journeys you make beyond the Lodge are not creative visualizations. They are more than mental projections. This is important, because the actions you take in these other worlds have a considerable impact in your everyday life. Your ego may attempt to undermine and resist this process, because it realizes that this path will lead to its own demotion, as your soul takes on a greater and greater role in your life. If you allow yourself to be interrupted while journeying, the results are very similar to what happens when you fall asleep while journeying – all the substance that was contained in your shamanic body is left where you were last connected with it. So it is best to make sure that your phone is turned off and that your housemates know not to disturb you.

So, here you stand, before the World Tree. You can feel the connecting energies flowing through you, the cord and the Tree. You can sense the shared substance from which your shamanic body is made. Now hold in your awareness the intention of journeying into the Upper World. Ask the Tree for guidance and permission to move through it, to pass between the worlds. This may require some patience, but eventually you will sense a shift, as if the Tree is opening a door in its trunk to welcome you inside. Take this as an invitation and enter the Tree. Hold the intention of moving into the Upper World and begin spiraling upwards, as if you were climbing a long spiral staircase. This spiral rises in a clockwise direction, which you will follow all the way to the top.

As you ascend through the Tree, you will eventually come to the shift between the Middle and Upper Worlds. This shift may feel rather subtle, like a scuba diver moving from deep water to the lighter, warmer surface layer. Just be aware of it, and begin to watch for the 'top of the stairs.' When you reach the top, you exit the Tree much as you entered it. You will find yourself on a broad limb emerging from the Tree, extending off into the sky. Welcome to the Upper World.

Having successfully arrived in the Upper World, you will probably want to do some exploring. Whatever your expectations, you will need to let go of them before proceeding. Expectations tend to get in the way of what the mind is already having difficulty grasping. Tune into the cord, which still connects you with the trunk of the Tree and then allow yourself to move outward from the center of the Tree, along the wide limb. The experience I have of this process is that the limb becomes wider and flatter until it seems like I am walking along a path. The rest of the landscape follows suit, becoming much like what you would see 'downstairs' in the Middle World. However, results may vary and it is best to keep a very open mind to take in whatever happens.

While the experiences arising from journeying in Upper, Middle or Lower World have much in common, they do have some differences as well. Imagine three layers of liquid of different densities. The most dense will sink to the bottom, while the least dense will rise to the top, establishing a clear separation between the three. The experience of the three worlds has much in common with this example. There is certainly a sense of greater density as you descend into the Lower World, and of less density as you ascend into the Upper World. Much of what you encounter in each World reflects this model as well.

Journeying back to the Lodge after spending time in the Upper World is simply a matter of reversing the directions. You return to the top of the Tree, where the branches emerge from the trunk, and connect to the substance of the Tree. Opening the Tree, you enter and climb down through the trunk, sensing the shift from Upper to Middle World. You emerge from the Tree when you reach the Lodge. It is a good idea to spend a little time in Lodge after returning from any journey. This helps to solidify the positive effects of the experience, while lessening any negative impact from coming back too quickly. It is analogous to a scuba diver coming up slowly from the depths, pausing at intervals to allow the body to acclimatize.

Journeying to the Lower World is essentially the same process, in a different direction. It is rather like you are entering a house in the middle floor and then moving up or down, depending on what you are looking for. You enter the Tree, and spiral down counter-clockwise, passing between the worlds, and exit beneath the roots of the World Tree, into what you may perceive as a dark cavern. The walls of the cavern open into various tunnels, all of which lead out into the rest of the Lower World, which most of us experience as very similar to the other worlds, with earth and sky and everything else you would expect.

Once you have experienced all three, you will be able to recognize both similarities and differences between the worlds. Besides the difference in density, one of the greatest differences between the worlds is in what you can find there. The Middle World is home to many nature spirits, including the more super-ficial (in terms of depth in the earth) land spirits, plant spirits, lesser animal spirits and those the Dagara call the Kontomble, the Irish call the Sidhe and which have a different name wherever you find them. More about them in the next chapter.

The Upper World, which as I mentioned above reflects the essence of your celestial soul, is perhaps the least concerned with the person you are now and the things that are important to you as an individual. The concerns of the Upper World and those who dwell there tend to be broader. Their perspective is very different and this comes across in our interactions with them.

The Lower World, which I personally find to be the most inter-esting, reflects your ancestral roots and the unconscious nature of all of humanity. This is also where the ancestral soul, as well as the souls of your ancestors, seems to be most comfortable. Other important types of spirit you will find in the Lower World are the great animal and plant spirits. Most natural animals, as opposed to domesticated ones, seem to engage in a form of group soul. The individual members of the soul may scurry about in the Middle World while they draw breath, but they are always in connection with their Great Soul in the Lower World, and when they die, they return to that soul. It is to this Great Soul that an aboriginal hunter prays before a hunt, to the spirit of the animal they seek.

When they take the life of one of the members of the soul, there are often rituals to assure its return to the greater animal soul. This ritual is usually as simple as pouring some of the animal's blood on the earth, along with a prayer of gratitude. Grandfather taught me a similar ritual to use when I come across roadkill. I reach out energetically to sense if the spirit is still lingering and then open a door into the Lower World and send it home.

There is a ritual that I often lead my students through toward the end of the Opening Inner Doorways weekend. We begin the ritual in Lodge, seated around the World Tree. Grandfather passes out seeds, small, round and hard. The students are instructed to come up with a goal for the ritual; something that they genuinely wish to bring into their lives. This purpose is then whispered to the seed, which is then placed beneath the tongue, where it will remain until the conclusion of the rite.

Stoppered gourds are passed out as well, which will be able to carry water from the Upper World into the Lower World. We enter the Tree together and climb into the Upper World, where I show them to a fountain of living water. Here they drink and fill their gourds.

We journey from the Upper World, through the Tree, into the Lower World, passing through the Middle World without emerging. Once in the Lower World, the students are guided to what Grandfather calls 'the garden where all things grow.' Here they are instructed to find a place to plant their seed, where they will water it and then return to the root of the World Tree. It was this ritual that gave me the necessary push to write and publish my last book, Dance of Stones.

I once asked Grandfather if the experiences I had while journeying were real. His response was:

Imagine you take a trip to a far off place, where the food, customs, clothing and language are all different, and then return home. As soon as you come back, your friends come to you and say, 'Tell us. Was it just like it is here?' This is really the question you are asking when you try to discern whether your experiences are real. The question you are really asking is, 'Is the place that I went to exactly like the one that I am used to?' This is the wrong question to ask. Instead, ask, 'Do my experiences in this other place have a lasting impact on my life? Do the changes that arise from the work that I do in this other place remain and continue after I return?' These questions speak to the validity and reality of the experiences in a deeper and more productive way. In my experience, the impacts on my life have been a deepening sense of equanimity and calm, a growing sense of compassion, both for myself and for others, and a profound shift in how I identify with self, soul and the world.

If you follow this path for very long, the validity and reality of the work will become self-evident.

Chapter 8

Medicine Body

When a client walks into my office, the first thing I do is to move into Medicine Body and extend my awareness to envelop them, offering gentle support and containment. As I do this, my Medicine Body becomes aware of the full spectrum of the client's energetic and physical presence, showing me where to direct my attention and the best approach to take toward healing.

I also use Medicine Body when performing ritual or ceremony. Moving into Medicine Body puts me into the proper state of consciousness, creates an energetic containment for the ritual, and also offers a subtle invitation for anyone else in the ritual to move toward a similar state.

All living physical bodies radiate energy on a number of wavelengths, from heat and magnetism to the more subtle energies of consciousness. Our bodies are constantly surrounded by this cocoon of energy, generally referred to as the 'aura.' The Medicine Body is what arises when the aura is charged with enough of the right kind of energy so that it can support consciousness beyond your skin. This energy is the particular kind of energy with which we think, feel, process emotion and connect with spirit. The Chinese, who have been working with and discussing energy for longer than most others, call this sort of energy 'shen.'

Our bodies naturally take in energy, or qi, from the food we eat and the air we breathe. Our bodies have three different dantien, or burners, which are involved in the process of digesting this undifferentiated qi into the forms of energy we use. The lower burner is located about 3 inches below your navel. This is where you collect the qi that you take in. Once in the lower burner, the qi is transformed into the kind of qi the body uses to make blood, muscle and other tissue. When there seems to be enough to meet the immediate needs of the body, the excess is sent up to the middle burner, located at the heart center, where it is further digested into the qi that directs the other processes of the body. The excess here is sent further on to the upper burner, located in the third eye, where it becomes the shen that we will send out through the crown of the head, into the aura, creating the foundation for the Medicine Body.

The Medicine Body is composed of three separate layers. Moving from next to the skin, outwards, these layers appear to correspond to the physical body, the emotions and mental state, and the soul or spirit. When all three layers of the Medicine Body are healthy and open, the physical, emotional and spiritual health of the practitioner is also apparent.

The successful practice of establishing and working with your Medicine Body has various benefits, both for yourself and others. Simply moving your attention into Medicine Body and sitting in meditation is revitalizing and cultivates the kinds of energy that we need to live healthy lives. The outer layers of our auras hold the 'blueprints' our soul carries for this lifetime. Whatever the reason, I have seen physical, emotional and soul-level healing arise just from this simple practice.

When Medicine Body is active, you will also have a heightened awareness of anyone sitting in its field. With some practice, you will become aware of the physical, energetic, spiritual and emotional states of anyone sitting in your field. As you gain experience, you will find that your awareness deepens.

Exercises to cultivate the Medicine Body show up in various practices from Peru to Tibet. While there is considerable variation, all these practices use a combination of breath, focused attention and physical techniques. The exercise below is similar to those used by some tantric and Tibetan Bøn traditions.

The exercise is complex and will take considerable practice to master. It includes breathing, mental focus, energetic manipulation and physical movement, all coordinated to amplify the body's natural production of shen.

Please be aware that this exercise can be dangerous for anyone with very high blood pressure. If you decide to practice the exercise and begin to feel pain or feel faint, stop immediately.

Since the exercise is complex, I will address each element separately and then bring them together. You begin with taking the correct posture. Sit with your knees lower than the top of your hips, your spine erect, your tongue resting lightly against the roof of your mouth. It is possible to do this seated in a chair, but probably best to use a cushion and sit on the floor.

Your breathing will be very important. Every breath will be an intentional part of the exercise. You begin with fire breath. This is a fast, relaxed panting breath, inhaling and exhaling through the nostrils by 'bouncing' the diaphragm. You need to breathe as fast as you can comfortably maintain this form while remaining relaxed. At the beginning, only do 60 breaths before moving to the cooling breath. Once you have had some practice, move that to 90 or 100.

The cooling breath releases any built-up pressure that may be dangerous. The cooling breath is a long slow exhalation, followed by a long inhalation through the nostrils, then exhaling through pursed lips, with the tongue still against the roof of the mouth. After the cooling breath, you will inhale slowly and deeply, through your nostrils, filling your lungs as much as is comfortable and then hold your breath and swallow. Hold your breath for as long as possible. When it feels like you can no longer hold your breath, take another short breath in, swallow again and hold a little longer before exhaling explosively.

Practice the breathing by itself a few times before adding in the next element, which is the physical action of opening and closing the body's natural locks or bandhas at your root, throat and crown. You close and open the root bandha, which is located at the perineum, by alternately clenching and relaxing the muscles of your pelvic floor, with the intention of opening and closing the flow of energy through this area. Closing your throat bandha is done by swallowing and then holding your breath. The crown bandha is mostly a matter of intention, unless you are capable of clenching and relaxing the tissue on your scalp.

While performing the fire breath and the cooling breath, you want your root bandha open and relaxed. When you take the deep breath in and hold it, you swallow, closing off the throat bandha. At the same time, you clench the muscles of the pelvic floor, closing the root bandha. Then you begin to alternately close and open the root bandha. When you can no longer hold your breath, you take a short additional breath in through your nostrils and immediately swallow, closing the throat bandha again, while keeping the root bandha closed. Then clench and relax the root bandha three more times before releasing the breath, with the root bandha held closed but the throat and the crown wide open, allowing the energy to stream upwards and out, into the space around you.

When you have practiced these two together, begin adding the physical movements that are a part of the exercise. On the second long inhalation, the one after the cooling breath, slowly draw your arms up to either side, continuing upward to clap your hands over head. You maintain this position while holding your breath. When you exhale, you lower your arms slowly to the sides.

With all the other pieces in place, add in your energetic focus. This begins in the lower burner, below the navel, while doing the fire breathing. With the cooling breath, you move your attention down through the root and up the back, over the top of your head and down through the front of the skull, passing through the roof of your mouth, through the tip of your tongue, which rests lightly against the roof of your mouth, and down the front of your body to the lower burner again. This is called the micro-cosmic orbit. You will follow the same path up your back with the next inhalation. When you reach the crown, you will move your focus up, out of your body, into the space about a foot above your head, between the palms of your hands, which are held above your head at this point. You will keep it here, while holding your breath and clenching and relaxing the root. When you finally exhale, sending the amplified energy upward from the crown, it will catch your energetic focus and expand it into the space around you. The sensation is reminiscent of a snow globe. Your energy and attention is shot up into the space around you, where it hangs for a bit before slowly settling back down to earth. With practice, the density of shen will increase, until it is able to sustain your continued awareness. At this point, you will have attained Medicine Body.

A simplified version of the instructions follows:

- Take proper posture;
- Focus attention in lower dantien;
- Fire breathing;
- Microcosmic orbit with cooling breath;
- Raise arms overhead and clasp hands above crown with rising breath;
- Hold breath and begin clenching and relaxing root;
- Exhale through crown as arms lower.

Having successfully created your Medicine Body, you will want to learn how to use it. The following series of exercises should help you to become more aware of your Medicine Body and allow you to also begin experiencing from the perspective of your Medicine Body.

Exercise One: This should be done with another person, who can offer feedback. The person should be sitting in the same room with you, close enough so that they will be contained within your Medicine Body. Begin by moving your awareness into Medicine

Body. Become aware of their physical body sitting within the layers of your Medicine Body. Be sure that you are completely surrounding them, containing them. Notice how this feels. Extend your awareness to their natural energy field – their aura. This will not be as extensive nor as dynamic as Medicine Body, but it should still be palpable through your Medicine Body. When you feel as though you have a clear sense of their aura, kinesthetically direct your energy to squeeze in a bit on their aura, as if you were giving it a hug. Check with your training partner and see if they can feel any shift in the energy.

An extension of this exercise is to reach down from your Medicine Body into the earth, providing a root for them. You can use the image of resting a golf ball on a tee. Once again, check to see if they have any sense of this.

Exercise Two: Once you are in Medicine Body, practice compressing yourself as tightly as is comfortable in toward your physical body. Notice any sensations, both physical and energetic. Now expand Medicine Body as far as you can while still maintaining cohesion. Practice alternating between these two extremes.

Exercise Three: Focus your awareness in Medicine Body and see what you can sense of the space around you. Try walking with your eyes closed and see what your attention is drawn to. Try this both indoors and out of doors. When you begin working with spirits, you can also use Medicine Body to heighten your awareness of their presence.

These exercises are an exploration of something that is a natural part of the human experience. All of us have access to what I am calling Medicine Body. Some readers may have already discovered it on their own. As you explore the Medicine Body, notice that it is composed of layers of energetic substance, which are denser closer to the physical body and becomes less so further out.

There are many ways to map these layers. What has worked for me is to define them as, beginning at the skin of the physical body and proceeding outward, physical, emotional and spiritual. I use these terms because it is clear that the closest and densest layer, immediately surrounding the physical body, is connected most directly with the health, function and well-being of the physical body. When someone is ill or injured, this layer will generally exhibit some indication of this, as a cloudiness, darkness or opacity, depending on how your mind interprets these things. The emotional layer tends to respond to any deviation from healthy, calm and open feelings. For instance, a person with chronic depression will usually exhibit an emotional body that is relatively thinner or more compressed than the other layers. The spiritual layer is an equally effective guide to assessing the quality of the person's connections with ancestors, Spirit and their own soul.

Medicine Body can be a valuable tool in assessing the physical, emotional and spiritual state of another person. It is less easy to perform such an assessment on oneself. We will explore more of the uses of this technique in a later chapter.

As with any other shamanic technique, ethical use is important. It is not good form to use your Medicine Body to influence someone without their permission.

Chapter 9

Working With Spirits

There is a strong tendency to consider anything that we run into while on a shamanic journey to be a psychological allegory, rather than a discrete entity, with its own agenda. It is difficult – perhaps impossible – to overcome this tendency. It is important what we think of these experiences, because our thoughts shape our responses to them. If we view them as 'real,' then we are more inclined to treat them with respect and honor. If we consider them nothing more than figments of our imagination, we are likely to treat them dismissively. This does not lead to a good foundation for a relationship.

In shamanic terms, a spirit is any sentient being that is not currently located in a living physical body. They may be encountered here in the natural world or on a journey into the shamanic realms.

The spirits we will be discussing break down into a few basic categories. There are nature spirits: those found in the natural world, such as land spirits, tree spirits and the ubiquitous Sidhe, known by many names in many languages; ancestor spirits – those who you are related to by blood and who hang out in the Lower World; helping spirits – those spirits who, by nature or choice, are in service to humanity; archetypal spirits – those arising from human belief and worship, such as abstract divinities, Santa Claus, the Tooth Faery, and synthetic spirits – spirit entities created by the shaman for specific purposes. There are also any number of spirits that don't fall easily into these categories. Spirits of the night are commonly found in many old cultures, and there are various means of protecting yourself from their mischievous or destructive intentions. Finally, there are also the spirits of humans who no longer have a living body, commonly known as ghosts.

The most commonly encountered, though mostly unnoticed, are the nature spirits. After all, they share the same world with us, for the most part, and we have moved into most of their territory, often destroying their homes in the process. Wherever you live, even in the most urban setting, there are spirits to be found. Anywhere that there are spirits, there is opportunity to begin developing positive relations.

You can find traditions for dealing with the 'little people' in most cultures. Simply leaving a bowl of milk or tea or food out in your back yard is a good beginning. Make sure to let them know that it is a gift for them though. They respond well to bells and to human voices, so it is usually sufficient to ring a bell and call to them, telling them that you are making a gift to them and ask for their blessings. Then you leave the offering for them and go away.

If you want to be a bit more engaging, you can purchase or build a spirit house for them. This is generally the size of a doll house and should be located so that the shadow of your own house doesn't fall upon it. The spirit house is offered in recompense to the spirits that live or did live on the land that has been taken up by your house. This then becomes a good place to leave offerings for the local spirits.

I got the idea from some friends who own an Indonesian import business. They gifted my wife and I with one for our wedding and it went with us to our new house, where we have lived now for over a decade. The house is made of molded concrete and brightly painted with earthy red walls and glittery blue roof. It sits in the back of our garden beneath a Japanese maple, surrounded by ferns and hastas, with a Buddha head resting in front of it. We used to have a strand of rope with several brass bells hanging from it that I would use to signal the spirits that a treat was coming, but the rope rotted away and I've not yet replaced it. The gifts I leave in the house are often from our kitchen garden, but the spirits seem to appreciate the occasional sugar cube or other sweets as well.

Once you have developed a practice of leaving little gifts for the spirits, you can ask for something in return. If they feel that you have respected them and are treating them well, they are generally happy to oblige with whatever help they can offer. They have a somewhat different perspective than humans, so can be helpful with finding lost objects and determining other unknowns, but they have their limits. Working with these spirits is a little like asking an Irishman for directions. They will be happy to help, even if they have no idea where you are going.

There is a similar practice you can use to connect with your ancestors. I cannot emphasize enough how important this particular practice is. Our relationship with our ancestors is what determines to a great extent how our life goes. Our culture has lost touch with this part of the human experience, and returning to it can heal many ills, especially addictive and destructive behaviors.

Set up a small table in your house, dedicated to the purpose of honoring and connecting with your blood ancestors. Place something on the table to represent your father's side and something to represent your mother's side. These can be photographs, old possessions of theirs or simply objects that you identify them with. The only guideline is that they feel right to you, that they be in balance with one another and that they fit comfortably on the table. In front of these objects, place a small bowl or plate. This is where you will place offerings. An offering is much like the present you would bring when going to visit someone. It is an acknowledgement of the relationship that you have and an indication that you would like to build and nurture that relationship. The same holds true for the offerings we leave for our ancestors. They may be specific to those ancestors we know. For instance: Aunt Sally always liked chocolate so I leave her a bonbon, or Grandfather liked smoking a pipe, so I leave him pipe tobacco. They can also be more universal, like a flower, a stick of incense or a drink of water. Many spirits also enjoy a wee dram, so a bit of whiskey rarely goes amiss, unless of course you know that your ancestors were against drinking.

Once you have established an ancestor altar, it is a good idea to visit it at least once a day for a few weeks, to build up the connection. A visit can be nothing more than a brief nod of respect, or it can be an offering followed by some time just sitting and listening, in case some of them have something they would like to share with you. To listen, just focus your attention on the altar, with the clear intention of being open to your ancestors. Depending on how active the link between you is, and how open you are to the link, you may find that messages come fast and furious... or not at all. Be patient, both with yourself and them. Continue to honor them and leave little presents. Their response may show up in other ways.

I go into the reasons why having a good relationship with your ancestors is a good idea earlier in this book, but I will go over some of the points here as well. Perhaps the most important reason is simply that we humans have had around 200,000 years of being in close relation to our relations, and we are rather used to it. Only in the past few hundred years has this broken down to the extent that it manifests as an invisible wound in our souls and psyches. This wound arises from a sense that 'someone is missing;' because the soul-level connection is not being reflected at the ego level. This has a number of consequences. Most forms of addiction and obsessive behavior can be addressed by developing the soul connection with ancestors, which indicates that the lack of this connection contributes to – or causes – the behavior. When these missing connections are recognized and honored, the addictive behavior fades.

Our ancestors are the spirits we have the strongest and most immediate connection with, and so they are an excellent place to begin working with the spirit world. We can learn a great deal just from setting up an ancestor altar and developing a regular practice of acknowledging and honoring them. We learn how to listen to and receive messages from Spirit; how to gift them with offerings to show our gratitude and appreciation; and, how to recognize their presence and influence in our daily lives. These lessons give us a strong foundation to work from when we move on to interacting with other spirits.

If you find that you are not getting the results you expect from the ancestor altar, you can journey into the Lower World to where your ancestors dwell and connect with them more directly, asking them for their blessings and letting them know that you have made an altar for them in your home, on which you are making offerings to them. This will tend to amplify the effects of the altar, as well as giving you the opportunity to meet and connect with ancestors who you may not have met during this lifetime, or not even known about before. Sometimes a particular ancestor will take an interest in you and begin to help out in your work. This is especially true if you happen to have a shaman in your lineage. This is not as unlikely as it may sound. Shamans tend to be born within the same bloodlines, sometimes skipping generations. Keep an open mind and be willing to let go of old family stories that may contradict the information that comes to you through these new encounters.

We can also develop good relations with the spirits of the land we live on. The spirit of the land, or land spirit, is tied to the specific piece of the earth, and its territory can reach for some distance in every direction. The territory of land spirits is usually demarcated by natural boundaries such as ridges, streams, and valleys. The nature spirits, those spirits who inhabit the surface of the land, can become attached to certain areas, but are not tied down in the same way.

While spirits are not exactly like humans, especially those spirits who have never worn a human form, there are some things we have in common. They appreciate courtesy and respect and will generally reciprocate what they perceive as good behavior. Of course, the same goes for bad behavior.

To build a relationship with the land spirit where you live, it is necessary to establish a stable connection. This can be done by setting a good sized stone at least a third of its length into the earth. Once the stone is planted, rest your hands on it and extend your energy and awareness through the stone and down into the earth. Keep going deeper until you feel a vibration or hum. Observe this for awhile. See if it responds to you. This is the Land Spirit. When you feel like you have its attention, let it know that you live on the land that is its territory and that you wish to have a good relationship with it, honoring its presence and asking for it to serve as a guardian. When it feels like you have been heard, offer your thanks and then pour a liquid offering over the stone. As with the little people, it is a good practice to check in fairly regularly with the Land Spirit, to maintain a good connection. This can be done by pouring offerings over the stone, with the intention of connecting with the land spirit and expressing your gratitude.

Helping spirits are a particular group of entities who have their own reasons for assisting the work of shamans. Some of them previously had human lives and have chosen to serve as teachers or healing assistants in non-corporeal form. Some have long established relationships with either the ancestral line of the shaman or with the shaman's celestial soul. These spirits will usually assist the shaman in recognizing and responding to the call to become a shaman in their current life, then help them to remember the teachings that have led them to shamanic practice in previous incarnations. Depending on their nature and talents, these helping spirits may also assist directly or indirectly in healing work.

Not all shamans have a pre-existing relationship with a helping spirit, but they can usually find one or more that are willing to offer their services. These are some of the most important relationships a shaman can have and they deserve a lot of attention. Whether the spirit reveals itself as having an existing contract with you, through either branch of your soul, or they are simply interested in assisting you in your work, you will need to get to know them in much the same way that you would a person you had just met, by spending time with them.

My primary helping spirit is the one I call Grandfather. He has been very active in my work with students and clients since the beginning, though he doesn't generally engage directly in healing work. He is more of a teacher, and is very present when I go on journeys in my shamanic body. He has let me know that he has some previous relationship with my soul, but has not clarified exactly what the nature of that relationship is.

There are other helping spirits I work with as well, but they are much less present to my everyday practice.

Though Grandfather tends to hang out in the Middle World, Lodge and Under World, most helping spirits are located in the Upper World. Journeying there with the intention of locating and engaging with a helping spirit usually bears fruit. Keep in mind that, like humans, not all spirits are equal. You may need to make many journeys before finding the spirit that is right for you and your work. Don't assume that the first spirit you encounter is the one you are destined to work with.

Consider that you may have an existing connection with a spirit from previous lives or through your ancestral line. It's good to start your search by checking for these connections. For ancestral links, look in the Under World. For past life connections, visit the Upper World. Upon arrival, state your intention aloud, then be patient. You may need to wait for a bit, but any spirit who has an existing contract will show up and make itself known.

If you do encounter an old friend, it is important to get to know them again, but also to discover what the nature of your agreement with them is. Contracts never go only one way. You need to understand what obligations you have to fulfill and make sure that you are willing to do so, or be prepared to renegotiate. Most spirits are willing to do this. If they are not, it's often best to walk away. After all, the contracts were between that spirit and the person you were in some previous incarnation, or with an ancestor, at a different time, with different cultural expectations. Sometimes the terms of the contracts are simply not appropriate by modern cultural standards. For instance, many of these spirit contracts stipulate regular animal sacrifice, which is practiced much more rarely these days. See if the spirit would be willing to accept some good rum or chocolate instead.

There are often taboos as a part of these contracts as well. They may be as simple as not eating pork, or so complicated that you wind up acting like you have an obsessive compulsive disorder. Be careful about what you agree to. Like humans, spirits are rarely completely altruistic. They feed off the relationship with you, so you need to set clear and healthy boundaries that they agree to abide by.

If you are one of the lucky ones who can hear what your spirit ally has to say and understand it clearly, that's great. For the rest of us, some form of divination comes in handy. Divination is often seen as fortunetelling, but it has historically been used to communicate with spirits, and it can serve you well.

There are many forms of divination. You will need to find one that works well for you; that you feel comfortable with and that your spirits are willing to communicate through. Personally I use a combination of different forms, depending on the situation. For detailed questions I use lot casting, which gives the spirits a wide spectrum of symbols to work with. Lot casting is a very ancient form of divination, using pottery shards, stones or pieces of glass with the aleph-bet inscribed on them. This practice has been recreated by the Am HaEretz movement in Israel and which I learned from my mentor Elisheva, the only Shophet of AMHA outside of Israel today. For questions that require a simpler answer, I use a pendulum or shells and stones. Over the years, I have practiced with many other forms, before settling on these. It will be up to you to determine what works best for you and your allies.

With practice – a lot of practice – you may come to the point where the spirits communicate with you through dreams, visions or directly in the shamanic body.

The relationship with your spirit helper or spirit ally is developed gradually. As with human relationships, it is not just the time you spend with each other, but your openness to one another that allows the bond between you to deepen. This openness is effected by much of what you are doing – things that are contrary to your ego's habitual way of perceiving. Eventually this erodes the ego's control over your sense of how things are and allows you to experience more directly. How long this takes depends on many things, but mostly upon the resilience of your ego. It takes a while to transform the part of yourself that has been responsible for monitoring what is real and what is not. There will probably always be at least some part of the whole 'you' that firmly believes that anything you cannot perceive with your physical senses is nonsense. The trick is knowing how to acknowledge and honor that part of yourself, without letting it run the show. After all, there are certainly times when healthy skepticism comes in handy. You will certainly need a dose of skepticism when dealing with spirits, because at the same time that you are trying to open your awareness to the non-physical reality of spirits, your mind will be trying to thwart your progress. What better way to do so then to provide you with manufactured images that tell you just what you want to hear. This sort of mental projection is very common and many credulous seekers waste years chatting with these rather than engaging with real spirits.

It is difficult to tell the difference, especially at first, between a mental projection and an entity with its own identity. This is one of the reasons it helps so much to have a teacher who is present in a physical body, so that they can interact with you on an ordinary level. While much can be gained from spirit teachers in the other worlds, it is very difficult to put the teachings into practice without some pragmatic guidance in the everyday world.

Chapter 10

Dream Body

Much has been written about dreams and the nature of dreaming, and I'm sure that there will be places where the teachings I offer overlap those of others. Much of what is written elsewhere focuses on the interpretation of dreams, which I will not be addressing, other than to say that observation is much more important than interpretation.

There are different kinds of dreams that we experience while sleeping. There are dreams in which you remain inside your own head and are essentially housekeeping for your psyche. These are important for the health of the ego, and can sometimes give clues to the workings of the unconscious.

There are also dreams in which you leave your own inner world, enter into your Dream Body and journey through the Dreamscape, where you encounter other dreamers.

Most people experience more of the inner dreams, only occasionally venturing into Dream Body. Further, when in either of these types of dreams, the dreamers are usually unaware. However, we also have lucid dreams – dreams in which we become aware that we are in a dream state. These lucid dreams can be either inner dreams or Dream Body dreams.

Since much of dream lore is covered extensively elsewhere, I will be focusing on teachings concerned with accessing the dream state and intentional movement into Dream Body.

There are several reasons to pursue your ability to dream lucidly and to direct your dreams at will. Dreams are a very effective means of receiving instructions from some teachers. They are also an effective medium for some kinds of out-of-body healing and ritual work. Most importantly, they are also training for the afterlife. When we die, our soul leaves our body and goes on a journey to the Lower World, where it will reside with the ancestors. The journey begins in a dreamlike state the Tibetans refer to as the Bardo. This dream is an opportunity for the soul to awaken and be able to choose their destination, or to go deeper into the dream and forget everything. With the dream practices during life, you can develop the skills and ability to awaken in the Bardo as well.

To enter the Dream Body while awake, begin by following the directions to enter your shamanic body. Once in Lodge, go to the circular wall around it and walk around, seeking the place where you intuitively feel the greatest connection with your Dream Body. Sit down here, with your back against the wall. There is a doorway in the space between where the tendons of your neck muscles attach to the base of your skull, where you can move between your shamanic body and your Dream Body.

Your Dream Body is already waiting for you. It is sitting against the outer wall of the Lodge. With your back resting against the inner wall, bring your attention into this doorway. Open the door and move through the wall of the Lodge and in through the same door at the base of your skull in your Dream Body. Shut the door behind you and expand into this new body. Notice any sensations of this body. You will still be aware of your shamanic body. (Indeed, you will still have some awareness of your physical body as well.) You can allow that to fade into the background as you focus your attention on the Dream Body.

The first few times you visit, it is enough to simply access this vehicle for your consciousness and explore its capacity for movement and perception. Once you can move back and forth freely, you can begin traveling through the Dreamscape, inter-acting with other dreamers.

What you will notice, upon returning to your shamanic body in Lodge, is that the shamanic body now feels much more dense and substantial than it did, at least by comparison to the Dream Body. With practice, the transition will become easier and your sense of being embodied will increase, adding to the substance of your dream experience.

One of the most powerful dream techniques I've received comes from Tibetan shamanic practice. In this technique you are moving into the dream state while fully conscious. This is a very powerful state of consciousness for any sort of transformative or ritual work. The actual technique is deceptively simple.

You begin by preparing for the practice by ensuring that you will not be interrupted or disturbed. Make a clear commitment to remain in the space and in the dream state until you are ready to emerge intentionally. This space should feel comfortable and safe. Examine the space visually. Look at the walls, the furnishings, any objects in the space. As you do so, begin considering how all of these things would appear if you were dreaming this. Imagine that the space itself is a dream, and that everything in it is a part of this dream – that you are a part of this dream. In an ordinary voice, say aloud: 'I am dreaming. I am in this dream. This dream surrounds me.' Look down at your hands, with the sense that you are looking at them in a dream. Feel the sensations as if they were in a dream. Speak aloud: 'I am looking at my hands in this dream. I am dreaming my hands. My hands are in this dream.' Then choose an object. Look at the object with the strong awareness that you are dreaming it, that it is in your dream. Continue your narration aloud, speaking of this object and then another, until you can feel yourself deep in the dream. The sensations of the dream state are of heightened sensual awareness, as if the air around you had become thick and electric. Your movements may become more fluid and soft, as you feel yourself moving deeper into the dream.

Once you feel yourself adequately engaged in the dream state, you can begin to explore. This is an excellent place to work on unfinished dreams, partially remembered dreams, or dreams that feel like they require resolution. It is also a powerful state in which to engage in ritual or other transformative work. This is partially because the dream state takes the ego 'out of gear.' It disengages the usual set of rules and regulations we live by, allowing for a much wider range of potential and possibility.

Enjoy the dream!

Chapter 11

Shaman as Healer

The role of a post-tribal shaman revolves around the practice of healing, in service to a community. The essence of this practice is called 'integration.' It is a process of gathering up all the pieces and putting them together in meaningful ways, so that they can awaken to ever greater levels of wholeness.

This leaves us to unpack what we mean by community, which is something very different for us today than it is for a tribal shaman. In tribal shamanism, this was a relatively simple process. The community was defined as the tribe. If you belonged to the tribe, then you were a part of the community. If you were not a member of the tribe, you were not covered by the shaman's services.

Our post-tribal culture defines community much more loosely, so that, when a shaman hangs up his or her shingle, they are in service to the community composed of those who come to them.[i]

Unlike the traditional community, the individuals who make up this one may have no other connection beyond their shaman.

Since the post-tribal shaman addresses wounds which cause or are caused by separation, healing is a process of restoring what was separated to its unified state. This is a very abstract way of looking at a process which is very concrete. However, it is important for the shaman to hold the awareness of that ultimate goal, even if he is working on plantar fasciatis in the moment. This is essential, because this work occurs on many levels simultaneously.

The post-tribal shaman must be able to observe, access and affect the fractal nature of her clients. This means reaching them on physical, energetic, spiritual and emotional levels. This is because the sort of healing a post-tribal shaman does is always about healing the soul, even if what he appears to be working on is only one part of this fractal. Every post-tribal shaman will develop strengths in different areas, which allows them to get a handle on their client's healing process by addressing the energetic, physical or emotional. The shaman's work is also limited by what the client is willing to receive. By maintaining the linkage between these different parts of the whole, the shaman can affect other parts, and the whole, by working with any of the different levels. In this way, working on an inflamed tendon can also begin the healing of the soul.

Most of what we recognize as shamanic healing techniques are means of accessing the different parts of this puzzle of Self and gradually piecing them together, bringing greater awareness at each step. In order to do this, the post-tribal shaman must be properly prepared and be capable of perceiving and holding the configuration of the client's integrated wholeness while still being able to focus in on whatever symptom or issue they are bringing to the process of the moment.

This preparation has several parts. The first piece that needs to be in place is a sense of health, balance and clarity. By this, I mean that the post-tribal shaman needs to be able to see and work with their own physical, energetic, emotional and spiritual issues to the point that they do not get in the way of the client's work. This includes everything from maintenance of physical health and not working while intoxicated to being very clear about personal and professional boundaries and making sure that the Qi is not blocked or congested.

In the same way that a doctor should make sure not to pass on illness by seeing patients while they themselves are sick, the post-tribal shaman needs to be aware of a broad spectrum of energetic, physical and spiritual imbalances that need to be adjusted before seeing clients. This is because much of the benefit of working with a post-tribal shaman arises from the subtle effects of sitting in the energy field of someone who is healthy, balanced and actively engaged with spirit. Much as a tuning fork can pass its resonance on to another tuning fork, the shaman passes on the vibrations of health, well-being and awakening to those in their presence.

The second piece is that the shaman needs to have adequate energy and the right kinds of energy to do the necessary work with their clients. This is achieved by following the necessary Qi cultivation practices, often a mixture of QiGong, Tai Chi or Yoga as well as regular sitting meditation.

The root of all this preparation is found in regular, daily practice. The daily practice should address all aspects of the post-tribal shaman – physical, mental and spiritual. The foundation of this practice is sitting meditation, which hones the ability to move between states of consciousness, journey and enter Soul Awareness.

Just as with any form of healing, it is important to clearly define what is within the post-tribal shaman's scope of practice. This will vary somewhat, depending on the nature of the shaman's other training. As a massage therapist, my training allows me to address a wide range of physical symptoms, but each of these is a means to address the deeper, soul-level issue that is the focus of my shamanic work. A shaman trained in psychotherapy might approach psychological disorders in the same way.

The post-tribal shaman needs to be clear of what he or she can effectively address, and what they cannot. Those clients with issues which lie outside the shaman's scope of practice should be responsibly referred to practitioners who can treat the client.

To be prepared to treat clients, the post-tribal shaman must also be aware of his own wounds, and be able to keep them clearly separate from the client. These are basic boundaries that have been developed in the psychological field, but they apply to the work of a post-tribal shaman and her clients as well.

This is a case history from several years ago in my practice.[ii] Karen came to me with symptoms of TMJ (jaw pain) and fibromyalgia. She had been referred to me by her dentist, but had not followed through until a friend of hers suggested she see me about her fibromyalgia. Since the two were not connected in her mind, it wasn't until she came across my card on a local bulletin board that she realized that both were sending her to the same person. She liked the idea of visiting one person to treat both problems, so she scheduled an appointment. Many clients who are coming for soul-level healing report similar stories of multiple referrals or of feeling 'led' to see me.

I begin all of my sessions by extending into Soul Awareness, so that I am observing from many levels at once and not merely responding to the client from my ego. In fact, I often have to catch myself when I think I know how to approach a treatment and am feeling clever because I've figured it out. In most cases, that is just my ego feeling pleased with itself and it is best for me to let go of that and look deeper for something beneath the surface, which my ego has missed. I have to surrender my desire to fix the client, to figure out their problem, and just sit and listen to what the soul has to offer.

At Karen's first session, it was apparent that the underlying issue was her own sense of powerlessness. She seemed nervous and somewhat fearful, though very expressive and highly energetic. She had a very lean body type and she sat perched on the edge of her chair as we talked, as if she wanted to jump up and pace the room. After listening to her symptoms and story for a bit, I asked her if she would like to get up and move some. Her mouth twitched slightly into a quick smile and she started to stand, before shifting back into the chair and responding that she 'really shouldn't.' I noticed that, as she did this, the tendons in her neck popped out, indicating that she was clenching her jaw. While my ego was noting that this may be a source of her TMJ, the soul was speaking.

'Who is it that would be bothered if you got up and walked around the room?' I asked. Karen blushed and her eyes shifted down and to her left. Her body closed in more on itself, her lips compressed into a thin line, and I could sense anger beneath the surface. She said she had no idea what I was talking about and I didn't push it, having already gotten the input I needed.

Karen chose to focus on the TMJ for our first session, so I had her lie on her back on my table and began to gently unwind the muscles of her jaws. Since I begin each session by expanding into Medicine Body, I was already resting in that awareness and using the connections with her energy to draw the tension down out of her face and neck. I began to sense that there was something besides the current stress stored in the muscles I was working, so I gently offered energetic support, like a deep root, to the tissue. As I felt myself moving into a deepening trance, Karen's head began to rock subtly back and forth. A moment later her eyes began to tear and she was sobbing.

'That's it,' I said. 'Just let it come up and out. You don't need to hold onto that any longer.' After a minute, she calmed and her breathing deepened, her muscles shivering slightly as they released the rest of the emotional charge. I sensed a deep stillness opening for her, and I reached out to connect with her ancestors. Her parents were both still alive, but I could feel them within her family soul, along with her grandparents and all the others who stood behind them. What caught my attention was that her father's face was turned away. As I focused on this, I felt a lump in my throat and a deep grieving, coupled with shame and rage.

With this vision of her father so capturing my attention, I asked her quietly how things were going between her and her father. 'He's good,' she replied. 'He is always kind of shut down – distant – but I know he loves me.'

'What do you think that's about,' I asked. I didn't see any issue between him and his own parents. It didn't seem to be something within the family that was causing this.

'Well, he was in Vietnam, in combat, for a couple years.'

'That would do it.'

I noticed her breathing was shifting again, becoming more shallow. I strengthened the root beneath her and with her ancestors and waited. This work involves waiting more than anything else, so developing patience is essential. It would be very easy to leap into mental gear and say what I THINK needs to be addressed, but experience has taught me that I miss most of the important substance when I do that. Instead, I sit with my attention resting in my lower dantien while still filling my Medicine Body as well. After some time I feel a subtle shift, as of things moving deep underwater, and something begins to rise to the surface.

'Try something for me, would you?' I asked her. 'Tell your father, 'Dear Dad. It is hard for me to see you in such pain.' Out loud – in your normal voice.'

'Dear Daddy,' she began. 'It's hard for me to watch you in such pain.' I could feel the emotional release building in her again.

'Continue, '...but I see now that you are strong enough to carry it on your own, and that you don't need my help...''

'But I see now that you are strong enough...' She took a shaky breath and continued. '...to carry it on your own, without my helping.'

'So I leave it with you now.'

'So now I leave it with you.' Her shoulders shook a few times and then she settled out, her breathing going deeper than before, her face relaxing completely. I waited a minute more and then set our energetic connection down gently and withdrew a bit, leaving the supporting root and containment of Medicine Body.

After that first session, Karen reported that her TMJ pain disappeared entirely and that the incidence of her fibromyalgia decreased. We worked together for a few years, delving through one layer after another, until it was completely gone. In the process, she came to know and appreciate herself much more deeply. While the pain she experienced had physical and energetic roots, it also had ones that reached into her soul. Until those were dealt with, her symptoms continued.

The soul wounds were somewhat apparent even in our first session, but it wasn't possible to dive directly into them. To do so would have been traumatic for her, only adding to her existing wounds.

Soul-level healing must move as the pace the soul sets. To move faster, or to move counter to the soul's current, only exacerbates the situation. There are many levels of connection, through love, loyalty, identification and shared trauma, which bind us to others and to our wounds. These webs of connection require careful unraveling so that what is necessary remains, while the rest is released. Sometimes this can happen in a single session, with a simple movement. It happens this way because the client is ready, which means that they have done most of the work for you before they came.

It is important to be attentive to what is going on at all levels of the client. Even the most subtle things can be clues. For instance, I noticed that when Karen repeated the soul sentences, she altered them slightly. It gradually became clear that this was because she needed to feel that she maintained her own identity around anyone she considered an authority figure. Changing a few of the words, or the sequence allowed her to do so, without getting in the way.

The shaman's best tools are ones that work on more than one level. An excellent example of this is Medicine Body. Like so many things to do with Shamanism, this one is ambiguous and thus difficult to explain in ordinary language. The way I describe it in workshops is the awakened aura.

Consider the human aura – a field of subtle energy emanating from and surrounding the physical body. Under normal conditions, this energy field serves to connect with the energies of the surrounding world and offers some support to the body's immune system. To amplify the aura, we use the body's capacity to digest and transform energy.

It may come as a surprise to some readers, but the Chinese figured this out at least 4,000 years ago, and they were not alone. The body takes in energies that are not directly useable, and processes them into forms that it can use. The process works much like our physical digestion. The energy digestion uses three different energetic 'organs' in the body. The Chinese refer to these as dantien or cooking vessels. The first is located just below and behind the naval. The second is just below the center of the chest. The third is in the forehead.[iii]

We take energy in all the time, from the food we eat, the air we breathe, and even from the environment around us. This energy enters through the soles of our feet, the palms of our hands, the crowns of our heads, and is drawn down into the lower dantien. Here it is processed into the kind of energy that our body can use to build all the tissues it needs to function. When the body feels that it has an adequate supply of this sort of energy, it moves the excess up into the second dantien, where it is further processed into the kind of energy that we use to motivate the various functions of our body and to think and feel. Finally, when this vessel feels full, the additional energy is moved on up into the upper dantien, where it is refined into the kind of energy we use to connect with spirit. This energy is then released into the area around the body, thus creating and maintaining the substance of our aura.

The Chinese also developed terms for the different kinds of energy. The energy we take in from the environment is called jing, this energy is transformed into qi which is used in many ways by the body and further processed into shen and then wuji. Collectively, all these forms of energy are known as Qi (Chi), so I will be referring to them as such.

In our daily lives, our bodies generate enough of the wuji to support our aura and protect us from disease. To create Medicine

Body, we amplify this process to build up the density of wuji in the aura and supplement it with shen, so that we are able to extend consciousness into the field surrounding the physical body.

This exercise is the same as I describe in the earlier chapter on Medicine Body. It is described in a slightly different manner here, which may be helpful to some.

If you have high blood pressure or heart disease of any kind, do not attempt this exercise. Important note: If you feel dizzy or nauseous during any part of this exercise, cease immediately. Breathe through your mouth and put your head between your knees.

Begin by taking a comfortable seated posture, with your spine erect and your knees lower than your hips. Rest the tip of your tongue against the roof of your mouth, directly behind your front teeth. Practice a panting breath through your nose, with your mouth closed. The breath should flow easily and evenly through both nostrils. You should feel as if your diaphragm is 'bouncing' up and down.

During this exercise, you will be drawing Qi along a path that runs up the back of your spine, over the top of your head and down the front of your body. Imagine this path as a line of light running in one continuous track up your back and down your front. You will begin by picturing a golf ball sized sphere of light at your lower dantien. Move this ball of light along the line of light, down between your legs and up through your sacrum and up your spine, over the top of your head and back down again. Cycle the ball of light a few times, until it seems to move easily and comfortably.

You will be using bandhas or 'body locks' at the perineum and throat to contain the Qi until you are ready to release it through the throat and up through the crown of your head. The root lock is performed by tightening the anal sphincter, as if holding back a bowel movement. Then clenching the urethra, as if holding back urine. Finally drawing the naval back toward the spine. You will be drawing pulses of earth Qi up into the body through the root lock by relaxing the anus and genitals, while keeping the naval drawn back, then clenching both again, with the intention of grasping earth Qi from the ground beneath you and drawing it upward into your lower dantien. Practice this until you can pulse the lock open and closed without tensing up the rest of your body.

The throat lock is simpler. The head is held erect, the chin drawn slightly downward. In this position, you will take a deep breath and then swallow, holding the throat closed as you contain the breath.

After performing these preparations, you are ready to begin. The nature of this practice is the amplification of the natural digestion of the Qi, which is then projected out into the space around the physical body, into the aura. Here it builds until a critical threshold is crossed, which allows this charged field to support consciousness similarly to the physical body. When this happens, the kinesthetic and proprioceptive senses expand into the aura, which becomes the Medicine Body. This is accomplished by the use of breath and energetic focus to hold the energy in the lower burners as it builds intensity, then releasing it to flood the aura with wuji and shen.

There are a few different things going on simultaneously, and you will have to monitor all of them. You will be controlling and using your breath, visualization, kinesthetic awareness and more to practice this exercise effectively.

You begin in the sitting posture, spine erect with tongue resting lightly against the roof of the mouth behind your front teeth. Your attention is focused on the ball of light in your lower dantien. Let go of any thoughts or sensations. Allow your mind and body to move toward Stillness.

When you feel you achieved a strongly concentrated focus, begin the panting breath, your diaphragm making a relaxed bounce as you breath rapidly through your nostrils. Count your breaths to at least 50 but not more than 90, before moving to the next step.

When you have completed these breaths, exhale through your nostrils while moving the ball of light from your dantien along the orbit. When you reach the perineum[iv] begin inhaling, continuing to move the ball of light upward through your sacrum, up along the back of your spine and over the top of your head. As you bring the ball of light over the top of your head, begin exhaling through pursed lips, your tongue still against the roof of your mouth. This is the cooling breath, and acts as a safety measure to keep your system from overheating.

As you slowly exhale, you draw the ball of light down along the front of your body to the lower dantien and continue on down, making another orbit. As you move through the perineum, close your mouth again and inhale through the nostrils. This time, as you draw the ball of light up your back with your inhalation, you will also be slowly raising your extended arms upward, palms facing upward, elbows straight, until your palms come together above the crown of your head. As your hands clap together, the ball of light leaps from the crown of your head upward into the space between your palms. At the same time, having inhaled deeply as you drew your arms upward, you swallow and hold your breath, with the intention of keeping your throat locked against any rising energy, so that it is contained in your lower burners.

With your focus held in the ball of light between your palms, begin alternately clenching and relaxing your root lock, drawing more and more earth Qi up into the furnace of your lower dantien. Continue this until it feels like you can no longer hold your breath, then take another quick inhalation through your nostrils and swallow once again. Clench and relax three more times and then, holding the root lock closed, open the throat lock and release the energy to erupt through the upper dantien and out through the crown of your head. As this fountain of energy bursts out the top of your head, open your hands and let the rising energy carry the ball of light up with it. Gradually lower your arms to your sides as your focus expands into the space around you, emerging from the ball of light as it dissolves into the charged atmosphere that now surrounds it. Remain suspended in this charged space as long as it will hold you. Until there is sufficient Qi to maintain it, the energy and your consciousness will tend to gradually fall back into your physical body, like the flakes in a snow globe settling back to the base after being shaken up. After several repetitions, the energy will build to critical mass and be able to continue to support consciousness until it is withdrawn, or until focus is lost and the Medicine Body collapses.

The Medicine Body has many uses, both for the individual as well as with clients. Individual use, as part of regular practice, promotes Qi production and flow, supports the immune system, eases access to Soul Awareness and helps the physical body realign with its energetic blueprint.

The use of Medicine Body with clients begins with providing a safe sense of containment and support. This is accomplished by expanding the Medicine Body to surround the practitioner and the client. Contracting the outer skin of the Medicine Body can then provide a sensation akin to an energetic 'hug.'

Holding the client in the Medicine Body provides the post-tribal shaman with a wide spectrum of data, ranging from a greater awareness of the client's physical state to a deeper perception of the emotional, energetic and spiritual issues arising within the client's field. It allows for a deeper level of engagement with the client, especially when the shaman engages Soul Awareness, which is also made easier by extending into Medicine Body.

Medicine Body is much more than what can be put into words. The experience itself is the best teacher. This is a technique that appears in many places around the world, because it is so essential to the human condition. Perhaps most important, it manifests the role of the shaman quite powerfully, because it produces the ambiguous state of being in two apparently contradictory states simultaneously. This is a fractal of the shaman juggling Soul Awareness and ego, infinite and finite, human and divine. This is one of the most accessible expressions of the paradox of shamanic practice.

The healing capacity of the post-tribal shaman is limited – and enhanced – by many things, including the capacity of the client to engage, receive and acknowledge the work. If the client is not ready, or is unwilling to move forward, it does not happen. I have had many experiences with clients where I lost sight of this for a while, and got frustrated, because I was following my own agenda rather than theirs. Fortunately, this happens only rarely now.

There are many areas in which wounding at the soul level can significantly degrade the quality of life. A good example is Post Traumatic Stress Disorder. There are some diagnosed with PTSD who respond well to talk or drug therapies. There are others who seem unable to lessen the severity of their symptoms beyond a certain point. The cause for this is often a soul-level wound, which is not being addressed by the existing therapies. I have worked with several veterans, all of whom responded very positively to the soul-level healing work. It was my own healing from PTSD, using these techniques, that led me onto the path of shamanism, so I feel a particular loyalty to others who suffer from similar wounding.

It is always important to keep in mind that Shamanic healing is not a panacea. It is certainly not a pill that can ease all pain, dispel all discomfort and cure all ills with no exertion on the part of the client. On the contrary, most find that shamanic work – done for oneself as a process of exploration and healing, received in treatment from a shaman, or offered as a shamanic practitioner – conjures up some of the most uncomfortable, terrifying and challenging experiences imaginable. In the end, the outcome is usually extremely positive, but only if the person has been willing to commit to the process, diving deep into whatever the journey presents.

Chapter 12

Soul Retrieval

The subject of soul retrieval can be broken down into a few major pieces:

- What do we mean by soul?
- How can this soul be lost?
- How do we go about retrieving these lost parts?
- What to do with the parts once retrieved.

The first part of this is the most complex and confusing, because those of us raised in the current Western culture have no understanding of what traditional cultures and shamanic practices refer to as 'soul.' Instead, we are generally raised on a vague notion that the soul is some part of us that is hidden from the view of our ordinary self and which only appears after death, to provide us with our reward or punishment in the afterlife. This simplistic perspective effectively alienates us from any real identification with the soul, which leads to further difficulties, as I will describe shortly.

From a shamanic perspective, and specifically from the view of a shaman working in our Post-Tribal culture, the boundaries of the soul are both difficult and necessary to determine. Difficult, because the experience of the soul is vastly more complex than the simplistic notion of angelic or demonic spirits wafting or plunging to their respective rewards. Necessary, because our ever-more rational minds require some degree of explanation for – some means of conceptualizing – the invisible workings of these nebulous parts of self to be able to make the leap into the surrounding territory.

To begin with, it will come as a surprise to most that there is more than one part to the soul. In shamanic practice we deal with at least three main parts: The egoic, the ancestral and the celestial. The 'egoic' refers to the parts of the self that arise in response to your presence in this physical body in this lifetime. By 'ancestral' we mean anything pertaining to the bloodline of our physical body in this life. By 'celestial', we refer to that part of the soul which has taken on other lifetimes, other bodies, before this and will likely be reborn many times more after this body dies.

The ancestral and celestial parts are grounded in the substance of Self that exists prior to the birth of the body, while the ego arises as an interface between these parts and the experiences of being alive in a human body in this place and time.

The ancestral can be further broken down into the communal and the individual. There is a way in which each of us is our entire family, at a soul level. The difference is similar to identifying with a whole neighborhood rather than a single house. At the same time, you also remain an individual within that communal soul. The individual aspect of the ancestral soul is what provides the body with its life force and vitality. The importance of the communal aspect to the soul is overwhelming. Our human experience over the past 70,000 years or more leads these deeper parts of us to expect that communal connection with our family, both living and deceased. Since our egos are not taught to honor these connections, or even that they exist, this expectation goes mostly unfulfilled, which creates a sense of profound lack, leading to addiction as we attempt to find what we are missing from our inner landscape in the Outer World. This perceived lack is a fundamental part of what I refer to elsewhere as the invisible wound.

While this sense of having many parts to the soul is common in traditional cultures, it is almost unknown among those living in the currently dominant Western culture. This is one reason why those in more traditional cultures often look on us with compassion, for having lost so much of what they hold as invaluable parts of the human experience.

The celestial soul is the part of us that has experienced rebirth through many lifetimes before this. In traditional cultures, this part would also be considered a part of the tribal identity, as it would have been reborn repeatedly into the tribe throughout many generations. Currently this kind of rebirth into the same family or group over many lifetimes is exceedingly rare outside those traditional cultures which still place greater importance on the communal aspect of the human soul than they do upon the individual.

It can be confusing to treat the ego as a part of the soul, but there is a sense in which we are using the term ego to describe the deeper part of the Self in the process of interfacing with the physical senses and, through them, the experience of being human in this world. From this process of taking in the data from the world around us and translating it into meaningful forms, we also create our own sense of identity in the world. This identity generally becomes ever more rigid with time and experience, unless it is regularly challenged by the deeper parts of Self, which we are referring to as 'soul.' When the ego is successfully broken down and reshaped by the soul's awakening, it can be integrated into the whole Self, allowing it to bear more resemblance to these deeper aspects of the Self rather than the influences of family, culture and mass media.

This is obviously quite a complex configuration of aspects, which are mostly relegated to the unconscious, leaving the ego to experience the objective world with little or no sense of the larger self that supports it. When the ego comes to realize that it is only a small part of a much larger self, it is generally a traumatic event, now characterized as spiritual crisis.

In addition to the trauma arising from a spiritual crisis, individuals can encounter any number of experiences during their lifetimes which leave them traumatized at physical or emotional levels. These traumas are the greatest cause of soul loss, and the incidence of this in our culture is so widespread as to be almost universal. When we experience a loss or an accident that is intense enough to leave us stunned, our ego has been taken off line and our soul often acts to limit the damage by ablating some part of itself to carry away some of the resulting emotions. These lost parts can be naturally reabsorbed, if the person remains near the place of trauma while they heal. Our soul, along with all the energy of our body, recognizes its identity with the rest of us and will seek to return if given the opportunity. However, when the person leaves the immediate area before they are ready to allow the lost parts back in, those pieces remain there until they can be retrieved.

In some cases, an energetic intrusion will take the place of the missing part of the soul. This presence blocks the reintegration of the lost part, and it must be extracted before proceeding. These intrusions are usually not difficult to remove, though at times they can be stubborn. This is best dealt with prior to the retrieval. Once the extraction has been performed, a 'packing' of the client's Qi is left in the wound to keep it from filling with any further foreign intrusion, which is then removed when the soul is retrieved.

The retrieval itself generally entails a shamanic journey to the site of the client's traumatic event, at the present time. There the missing piece is accessed and welcomed back into the shamanic body of the client. The shamanic body is lead back to Lodge and then the client is instructed to bring the newly retrieved substance back with them as they return to their physical body. Clients usually report a sense of fullness; of being more substantial, upon returning.

Because this is a post-tribal technique, and the clients have egos that are individuated from the community, emphasis is placed on empowering the client through the experience. This means that it is necessary to engage the client throughout the process, so that they have a feeling of personal accomplishment afterwards, rather than a sense that they have been 'fixed' by the shaman. This differs from many traditional soul retrieval techniques, which leave the client resting comfortably in their body, while the shaman stalks and retrieves the lost parts, then sends them back into the client's body, and in some cases, even facilitates the integration process. While this is appropriate in a culture in which the communal soul is still dominant, it can be damaging to the individual identity in our own culture. Since we value the individual so highly, placing the client in a position where they receive such an important experience, which they cannot reciprocate, can often leave them feeling disempowered – the opposite of our intention.

This is the essence of soul retrieval: The extraction of any intrusions which have taken the place of the lost soul parts; identifying, locating and retrieving the lost parts; and, the integration of those parts back into the whole self.

One variation on this practice is to journey through the client's body to their internal landscape, where considerable healing work can be done, including the retrieval of many lost soul parts.

Chapter 13

Healing the Invisible Wound

When I speak of the 'invisible wound', I am usually referring to that gradual separation that has occurred over the past several hundred years, between our individual souls and our communal souls, between ourselves and the collective whole of our communities; between our thinking minds and our souls; between our ordinary egos and the whole realm of Spirit, earth and the divine. There was a time when I imagine humans lived in a world in which they lived all of these connections more fully. In this imagined world, their egos and souls were almost indistinguishable and their lives were deeply satisfying, though they would seem very limited from our modern perspective. We see echoes of this in some of the remaining traditional cultures, where the ancestors are still revered and acknowledged and the pursuit of 'happiness' has not completely eroded the natural contentment of lives well-lived.

This wound shows up between our ego – our perceived self – and our ancestors. It arises as an unidentified, usually subconscious longing for connections that our souls expect to find. Our souls – these deeper parts of Self – have experienced thousands of years through many lifetimes, in which the connections were there, and have developed an understandable expectation that they will continue to be there. When they are not – when our ancestors are forgotten and we cannot feel the earth – then we feel instead a deep hunger, which cannot be fed without awakening to these wounds and working to heal them. Instead, our egos reach out to whatever is available to calm the inner hunger. This leads to drug abuse, alcoholism and various other unhealthy pursuits.

This invisible wound appears at every level of our existence.

On the level of ordinary, everyday life, the invisible wound shows itself in the form of addictive behaviors, ranging from alcoholism and drug addiction to over-eating and workaholism. There is no one who I have met, raised in our culture, who does not exhibit this wound to some extent. For many, the wound is not deep enough to bring on the symptoms of addiction so strongly that they become dysfunctional, but the hunger is still present.

This level of invisible wound, this deep separation, is the result of the breaking down of a more integrated and conservative way of life. By integrated, I mean that all the parts were connected and knew themselves to be connected. By conservative, I mean that, rather than each generation wanting more than the one before, they wanted to remain the same. Generation after generation were born, lived and died within walking distance of the bones of their ancestors. They knew the land they lived on intimately and relied on it for their survival. Their ancestors were with them in the wind, the stones, and the trees. They identified more with the communal sense of 'Self' than with the individual self.

Healing the invisible wound is Soul Retrieval on a large scale.

The celestial souls of these traditional tribal groups tended to be reborn into the same clan generation after generation, leading to a deeply integrated sense of community. This practice continues today in traditional cultures and in some rare cases in families with strong tribal ties.

The breakdown happened gradually, and had many causes. Population pressure eventually made it necessary for new generations to move beyond the ancestral lands to support themselves. These same pressures, combined with climate change and natural disasters, resulted in conflicts when one group's territory encountered that of a different and unrelated group. Sometimes these conflicts resulted in the eradication of a community, which meant that those souls could no longer be reborn into what they recognized as their proper place. It also meant that those ancestors no longer had descendants, providing them with a living connection with the everyday world.

I believe it was these changes which lead to the evolution in cultural and individual identity, from the communal to the individual. This singular transformation, from a culture in which every member of the group identified first and foremost as the group, to one in which each person identifies themselves as an individual and then as a member of many overlapping groups, has led inevitably to the underlying sense of dissociation and alienation, epidemic in the last several generations. They have thus led as well to the outer manifestations of the invisible wound.

Consider all the ways in which we still show the signs of our heritage as communal souls. In many cases, these left-overs of tribalism show up as problems, because the 'us and them' tribal mentality doesn't cooperate well with others, and doesn't lend itself to individual endeavors. Many of the elements of racism are little more than these tribal instincts arising in incompatible ways. It can be seen more subtly in the desire many people have to align with those they identify with, in everything from the choice of schools to favorite sports teams.

We no longer live within walking distance of where the bones of our ancestors are buried. We have lost that physical proximity with the place we – in the sense of our blood family – come from. This fractures the communal self, which is still present at a soul level, and leads to the sense of not belonging so common among modern individuals. In my work with clients over the past couple of decades, I have seen that, by bringing the ancestors back into spiritual proximity, the most violent symptoms of addiction begin to diminish and often disappear entirely. We create this sense of Spiritual proximity by setting up an ancestor altar in our living space, with photographs or symbols to represent our mother and father and the generations behind them. By honoring the ancestors through these symbols, through making offerings and asking for their continued blessings, we open lines of communication, drawing them closer to us and to our everyday lives. This is a powerful means of beginning the healing of the soul and its invisible wound. However, this is only dealing with the superficial causes and manifestations of the Wound. There are much deeper levels yet to explore.

At the core of the Wound is the separation between Self and Other, in the primordial sense. As Grandfather tells it:

Before the beginning is the One. Floating effortlessly in the void, it exists both only in itself and in reflection in the void. In seeing its reflection, it flees into the void. As the One and its reflection flee from one another, they create space, which in turn creates time. (If that is not self-explanatory, you might want to have a quick chat with your favorite physical scientist.) Because the two ends of the One are still connected, their flight is akin to stretching out a rubber band. Eventually it wants to contract again. This manifests as a yearning in the One for its now separate part, which leads it to seek to reunite with the Other. The One moves through what is now space and time, in search of its Self. When it encounters its reflection, it attempts to merge, only to discover that through the process of flight it has polarized into matter and energy, and can no longer simply merge back into the One. Instead, the part that has become matter feels force acting upon it for the first time, while the part that has become energy feels itself contained for the first time. Both of these experiences are the ground of consciousness, further separating the One from the world it has created and forming the ground of what we experience as reality.

This primordial separation of the One from Itself is the foundation of space, time, matter, energy, consciousness – everything that we experience as the world, through the physical senses. This separation is also the source of the invisible wound. Our whole existence is grounded in the wounded state of the One, and so this wound is reflected in every level of existence. Inherent within this is the knowledge that this wound can never be healed. As long as there is existence, the wounded/separate state of being persists. Only through the whole of existence collapsing into the unified state of One can the wound be healed. You could even go so far as to say that existence IS the wound.

Through the fractal nature of the world, we see the pattern of this wound, not only at the level of our personal separation from our soul, ancestors, earth, et al., and at the level of the primordial split of the One, but at every level in between as well. This fact forms one of the inherent Mysteries of our existence, and is reflected in the myths of many lands.

It would be understandable to give up at this point and simply acknowledge that we exist in a wounded state, which cannot ultimately be healed, since as each level is reunited it reveals a deeper level of wounding. The post-tribal shaman, however, carries the gift of paradox. Just because the wound cannot heal does not mean that it cannot also be healed. By experiencing the part of Self which is still in touch with the unwounded One, we are both wounded and unwounded/healed.

This sleight of hand trick is accomplished by being able to enter into the Awareness of the Soul. Soul Awareness is that state that all of us have some taste of when we first are born into our physical bodies, before the ego develops. During this time, we have difficulty distinguishing between Self and Other. This state of Awareness is still engaged in some way with the One, and provides us with a powerful tool for unraveling the Mysteries of our existence.

I have tried to express this as simply as possible, so many of the variations on the theme, the dance of unity and duality, have been left out. Direct experience is the best tool for realization. Just as you create an altar to your ancestors to heal that part of the invisible wound, you can set up a separate altar dedicated to the One Center. This is a good place to do your daily sitting practice as well.

Chapter 14

Shadow Work

Grandfather has been very dismissive about many spiritual paths, because they focus on the Light, and ignore the dark side of the work. This sort of path became very common with the rise of the 'new age.' Grandfather says that anyone who focuses so strongly on their ideal self, will be eaten by the unrealized self.[v]

The human experience is focused through the lens of our identity. This identity is formed by everything and everyone that we encounter and by how we learn to interpret these encounters. These experiences – of family, school, media and friends – shape our minds into the knot of self-perceptions we call ego. In many ways, this process is one of sculpting identity from the raw material of Self.

Notice we are not looking at ego as synonymous with Self, but as something created from that larger whole. This is done by repeated acts of identification: I am this; I am not that. Each time we own a piece of the Self by identifying with one part of it, we are excluding its apparent opposite, and forming the foundation of Shadow.

By Shadow, we are specifically referring to the 'not I' – to the conglomeration of all the parts of Self which we have identified as other than who we are. The ego is made up of many parts, and yet when healthy, it functions as a coherent whole. The Shadow has many pieces as well. These pieces have some influence as a whole, but it is in their individual forms that they seem to have the greatest impact in our daily lives. These individual shadows are generally formed by a traumatic rejection from the identity by ego. This exclusion polarizes the rejected parts relative to those which are accepted, creating a powerful charge that can ultimately be quite destructive.

To grasp this more deeply, it is important to understand that this whole process is fueled by our need to belong. It is fear of NOT belonging which causes our egos to throw out – dis-identify with – parts of the Self. Belonging is, after all, a matter of survival. For our ancestors, being cast out of community would usually lead to death. It has only been in the past few hundred years that social evolution has led to individuals who are capable of coping with the stresses of living outside of community, as well as the technology to be able to fend for ourselves without the support of others.

Imagine a young child who wants attention from her mother. This is a natural and inevitable part of the child's self-expression. However, if the mother is stressed and angry when the child approaches her, she may lash out in a manner that clearly communicates to the child: 'This behavior is not acceptable.' The child unconsciously accepts this and immediately begins to transform, relegating that behavior to the Shadow.

What is fascinating is the degree to which this Shadow, which has been excluded from the child's perception of herself, will continue to dictate her choices, actions and attitudes. Because the need remains as a part of the greater Self, even when it is consciously denied, it still yearns for fulfillment. This will lead the child, as she grows into an adult, to continue to seek attention surreptitiously, often embarrassing herself by actions that she doesn't really understand.

This work is so important because Shadow continues to influence and affect us, without our knowledge. If we walk a spiritual path that does not include welcoming back the disowned parts of Self, we are doomed to be consumed by those parts.

Shadow often shows up as blind spots – those areas that we tend to habitually overlook in our daily life and especially in our interactions with others. Blind spots are generally indications of a deeper Shadow at work that is blocking or distorting our perception.

The work of identifying, locating, and reintegrating our Shadows is a significant part of the post-tribal shaman's work, both for the shaman as well as for his or her clientele. This is a difficult process, made more difficult by the nature of both the work and of what is being sought. For the post-tribal shaman's personal work, this means relying to a great degree on spirit allies to identify and locate the Shadows, while with the client's work, the work is more direct, but also very challenging to the client. This work can also lead to considerable projection on the part of the client, so it is important to maintain as much clarity as possible.

For every Shadow we uncover and reintegrate, there are usually a few more lurking beyond our awareness. The work of tracking them down and bringing them back into the fold is a gradual process, but one that is as valuable as it is difficult.

To list all of the techniques I've used in this practice would take up most of this book, so I will focus on a few that are usually quite effective. These are focused on self work, rather than with another person. I will address those as well below. Many Shadow techniques have much in common with soul retrieval, in that they are tracking down lost parts of the self in order to re-unite them with the whole. What differentiates Shadows from lost parts of the soul is that the Shadows often develop a persona of their own, and may not come back toward wholeness as easily as parts that have merely been temporarily misplaced.

Doppleganger: Begin by moving into Lodge and shamanic body. Take some time to become very focused into your shamanic body and clear on how you look, feel and sound there. Your intention will be to journey to the Lower World, in search of a Shadow which is ready to be reintegrated. As you focus on this intention, speaking it aloud in Lodge, feel your connection with your Shadow in the Under World like a rigid beam emerging from the tree. Begin walking counter-clockwise around the World Tree, pushing into this connection as if you were winding the spring of a clock. This builds a charge between you and your Shadow. This charge will help you find and recognize your Shadow in the Under World. When you feel ready, enter the Tree and spiral down into the Under World. Once you emerge below the roots of the Tree, take a moment to get your bearings. Sense the polarized charge that connects you with your Shadow. Once you feel it, head in that direction. If you like, this is a good time to use a drum. Eventually the charge will bring you into proximity with your Shadow. It will appear as a photographic negative image of you; literally a shadow version of your shamanic body. The approach may require some coaxing, or even a bit of a chase, but as soon as you touch one another, the charge will be grounded and you will need to hold on and get it to listen to you. You will need to convince it that you are ready to welcome it into your identity. Depending on its nature, it may come willingly or it may resist for a bit. Because of their nature, all Shadows want to return to their true selves, whether they realize this or not, so the outcome is already determined. It's just a matter of getting there.

Black Mirror: For some Shadows, it is effective to go into Lodge and make a mirror set into the World Tree. Speaking aloud in Lodge, invite the Shadow to appear in the mirror. Once the Shadow is present, simply touching the surface of the mirror will draw it through and into you. The integration process is the same, regardless of the technique used to find and connect with the Shadow.

Evocation: This is a more advanced technique. You should practice with some spirits first. You create a safe defined space in whatever physical setting you will be working in. This can be done by laying tape on the floor, drawing a design with chalk (circles and triangles are generally most effective) and using your energy and intention to make it impossible for the Shadow you are calling to exist beyond the confines of that shape. An even simpler solution is to use a chair that is similarly charged. Once the space is set, begin calling to the specific Shadow that you wish to engage with. Be sure to let it know that it can only manifest within the space that you have defined.

Once you have a sense that the Shadow has 'shown up,' you can speak to it and begin a conversation. Address it directly in the space, or on the chair, and then step into the space or sit in the chair and allow it to speak back to you using your own body and voice. Go back and forth, being sure to leave the Shadow in the defined space, but moving closer to it with each exchange, until you feel ready to break the separation of the space and welcome the Shadow back into yourself.

Constellation: The effect of this technique is often stronger when applied for a client, perhaps because we are too close to our own Shadows to see them very clearly. You take some stones – I like to use some smooth river stones that I've collected over the years – and choose one to represent yourself and one to represent your Shadow. Place the one representing yourself where it feels like it belongs on a flat surface in front of you. Place the Shadow stone, naming it as well. Observe the relationship between the two stones, how they are placed? Do you have a sense of which direction they are facing? Do you have a sense if they are aware of each other?

Take time to explore the nature of the two stones, touching them from time to time and 'asking' them how they feel. You may be amazed at the quality and quantity of the input you get. Always keep in mind the intention of eventually having the stones move together, discharging the Shadow into the stone representing yourself.

These techniques use the nature of the shamanic realms to do the work that the conscious mind is unable to in this case, namely the identification and locating of the disowned parts of self.

Chapter 15

Ceremony and Ritual

In post-tribal shamanism, we define ceremony and ritual as distinct practices. Ceremony is a set of actions designed to celebrate, honor or acknowledge what is. Ritual is a set of actions designed to cause a change in what is. Sometimes an event can be both ceremony AND ritual.

We can use ceremony to honor the ancestors, acknowledge a rite of passage or celebrate a life – or death. We can use ritual to initiate changes we desire in our lives.

The most well-known shamanic initiation is probably the Vision Quest. It is also widely misunderstood. In most cultures that practice such a ritual, it is a rite of passage – a ceremony – an opportunity for the young person coming of age to connect with the spirits of their ancestors and the land they live on, to receive wisdom and blessings to carry them forward into their adult life. This ceremony reflects the change that is already taking place, and connects with supportive resources as it acknowledges the transformation that is occurring. It is not a ritual, because it is not MAKING the change happen. It is only celebrating it and, at best, helping to focus the process.

A similar ritual is often used to bring on a shamanic apprentice's full powers. After considerable preparation, they are sequestered alone for at least a day and a night. The circumstances of the setting are tuned to their own needs, personality and gifts, but it is usually in wilderness. They use the ordeal to connect with the spirits who will be helping them on their journey as a shaman. This is not a ritual to undertake lightly. It can have terrific benefits, but it can also be exhausting and sometimes even damaging to the initiate.

Another popular ritual or ceremony is that of the sweat lodge.

This has many variations and is often employed as part of the preparation for another ritual, for cleansing from something that has injured the participant, or as a ceremony of prayer and gratitude. It has a powerful impact, whatever its use, and must be experienced respectfully and responsibly.

One of the most intense shamanic initiations is that of Death and Dismemberment. Since much of the Shaman's work deals with the realm of spirits, it is essential to be able to engage with them as strongly as possible. This often entails leaving the physical body and experiencing physical death. It is also essential to not be too strongly identified with the ego. This initiation also greatly decreases this identification and works to dissolve the ego.

There are many ways to approach transformative ritual, but it helps to have an overarching strategy – a perspective that allows you to understand how and why each element is applied. My own strategy in creating effective ritual is this simple formula:

Intention + Energy Source + Bracketing + Shaping = Outcome

To engage in a transformative ritual is to have a clear intention to bring about a change in yourself or the world around you. Without a clear intention, the energy expended in the ritual is poorly shaped at best – if at all – and the whole effort is wasted. So the first element of effective ritual is intention. This intention may be a new job, a better relationship, fewer headaches or world peace. For this intention to be achieved, there must be a source of energy to cause the change. If an appropriate energy source isn't provided and designated, the ritual will draw energy from the most available source – generally you. The energy source could be a communal fire, dance, the earth, the ancestors or the life force of a stand of trees. If possible, the energy source should be complementary to the intention of the ritual.

Once these first two elements are in place, they must be clearly contained in a way that keeps the energy concentrated on the task at hand. Bracketing refers to a clear beginning and ending of the ritual, as well as clearly defined space in which the ritual takes place. The shaping process of the ritual may then begin, proceeding in a way that reflects the intention and respects the boundaries of the ritual. When all these pieces are effectively put into practice, the outcome has the best chance of resembling what you had in mind.

Applying this simple equation is an art. It can be used for any ritual, from the most simple to the most elaborate. Beware of situations where the structure of the ritual is defined more by social needs – 'We must find a part for Jim, or he will be hurt!' – than it is by the intention of the work. Another pointer for good ritual: Never use a script that you have to read from during the ritual. Either memorize the lines or extemporize. Reading from a page during a ritual is deadly boring.

Chapter 16

Preparing for Death

Immortality is composed of equal portions of Life and Death.
– Grandfather

Death of the physical body is an interesting issue for the shaman. Shamans usually undergo a variety of initiatory, transformative experiences which allow them to leave the body and the ego at will and to travel into the realm of the ancestors. This gives them perspective on the process of death and dying that is radically different from that of the uninitiated.

There are many parts that make up the Self. Some of these parts survive physical death, while others tend to die with the body or shortly after. The basic shamanic practices of preparing for death and dying tend to focus on identifying more with those parts that naturally survive the experience, while identifying less with the part that doesn't survive.

This leaves the individual feeling less fear and loss when considering the demise of those parts with which they no longer identify strongly, along with a sense of impending adventure as they prepare to go beyond the experience of this lifetime, into something Mysterious and larger than Life – in every way.

Some practices go beyond this basic goal, working to integrate all the parts into those which survive, and to train the mind to awaken after death, allowing for continuity of consciousness from one lifetime to the next.

What many do not understand is that rebirth from one lifetime to another is rarely a matter of conscious choice. The experience of the mind between lifetimes is dreamlike and, as in dreams, it is easy to get caught up in the situation as it appears, forgetting that it is a dream. When this happens we are drawn into our next lifetime through that dream, guided by our karma – the influence of our past actions. It is only by waking up within that dream – realizing that we have died and that we are in a disembodied state – that we can make a conscious choice about where we go from there.

With the deepest practices, the goal is to so fully integrate the whole Self, including the physical body, that the soul is capable of taking it all with it when it is ready to move on. The Tibetan Bøn Shamans refer to this as the Rainbow Body.

The foundation practice is simply resting in Soul Awareness. This experience of non-dual awareness allows us to disengage somewhat with ego and to relax into the larger experience of Self. Just sitting in Soul Awareness for a minimum of 20 minutes a day, preferably about the same time each day, will gradually bring about the dissolution of ego identification. It's not that the ego goes away for good, but it does drop out for awhile and, when it comes back, it more closely resembles the soul.

A more dramatic and traumatic means of ridding oneself of identification with ego is the shamanic initiatory practice of Death and Dismemberment. With shamans, the first cycle of soul awakening often entails intense visions of the body being torn open, cut apart and the entrails and internal organs removed. In most cases, they are replaced by objects that fulfill similar functions but from a different paradigm. In my own experience, my innards were replaced with beautifully glowing gems, each of which had an intelligence that supported my physical functions in some mysterious way. My sense is that these replacements are indicative of the increased role of the soul as the body/ego is reassembled.

Whatever technique is used, there is a cycle that develops, in which a charge to awaken builds which is resisted by the ego. Once the charge reaches critical state, the ego is released, destroyed or otherwise set aside to allow the soul to emerge more fully. This is followed by a period of often ecstatic or blissful awareness. At some point, as the individual begins to engage with others and their physical surroundings, the ego begins to reform. With each cycle, the ego is less defined by the past experience of this lifetime and more by the soul.

Once you are able to enter and rest in Soul Awareness at will, you can begin extending this practice to simple movements of the body. The idea is to remain in Soul Awareness while moving. It helps if you have some movement, like a Tai Chi form, that you have memorized, so that you can practice it with a minimum of conscious thought. Doing this can be difficult at first. It is common to be drawn into more conscious engagement with the movements. It is also possible to become disoriented and even nauseous. These obstacles pass with time.

Develop this practice until you are able to make even intentional movements with a continued Soul Awareness. When you are comfortable with this level of integration, begin expanding to using your voice. Begin with meaningless sound – humming or resonating – feeling the sensations while remaining in Soul Awareness. Continue with this, introducing memorized words – a chanted sutra or mantra.

What you are doing is increasing the level of engagement of your soul with your ordinary life, through integrating the sensations of movement and sound into Soul Awareness.

Once you have become competent in these practices, begin expanding to informal practice, outside of your normal meditation practice. Find times during the day when you can engage Soul Awareness. It is best not to do this while driving a car or operating heaving equipment, but for most of your daily routine, you should be able to do this readily. Even your thoughts can arise now, while maintaining Soul Awareness.

Focus on bringing yourself to Soul Awareness several times during the day, perhaps at particular times or whenever you perform a regular action. What this does is begin to train you to realize your soul in the midst of the ordinary routines of your day. Eventually this will allow you to realize yourself and return to Soul Awareness even after death.

I will address the teachings of taking your physical form with you at death only briefly, since while I have received them, they require initiations and experience which a book cannot provide. This practice rests on the realization that all that we identify with as self arises from the One Center – from the soul. When we are able to engage the level of Soul Awareness from which all the rest of Self arises, we can also draw these elements of self back into the level from which they arise, effectively releasing all form and energy, returning to pure awareness. The visible outcome is that the body dissolves into light, leaving only hair and nails behind.

Less ambitious is the intention of awakening in the after-death state, in Soul Awareness, with the ability to choose your next incarnation, with greater continuity of consciousness. In other words, being able to remember THIS life, after being born into your next body. One of the practices that leads to this is much like that of lucid dreaming. You develop the ability to wake up in your dream and realize that it is a dream, which gives you the opportunity to direct the dream. The after-death practice is the same. You wake yourself up in the dream-like state of afterlife and realize that your body is dead. You then have the opportunity to choose to remain in spirit form or to take on another body.

When a client approaches me to help them prepare for death, either as a rapidly approaching experience due to illness or old age, or as an eventuality, I share as much of this practice with them as they can use. For most it is enough to realize that there is more to them than their ego and their physical body, and to begin softening the identification with these parts of the Self. Some seek to delve more deeply into the Mysteries. I usually recommend that they attend the post-tribal shamanic workshop series, as these teachings are embedded throughout.

The experience of moving into your shamanic body and

journeying to the Lower World to speak with their ancestors has a very positive effect on those seeking a deeper understanding of our nature, both during our lives and after death. Grandfather describes it:

> When a person dies, their soul goes on a journey. If they are in a good relationship with their ancestors, some of them will be waiting when the body dies to help them on this journey. When they arrive in the Lower World, they are given a place among the other ancestors. Here they rest, looking at the actions and choices that made up their life. If there are burdens, they try to let these go. When this work has been done as well as it can, the soul splits. Part of the soul remains in the Lower World an individual within the ancestral soul. It will stay here for several generations, until it gradually dissolves into the communal soul of the ancestors. Part of it rises up through the World Tree, into the Upper World. Here it emerges like a little bird. It is very hungry and alone. It looks down into the Middle World, seeking in the way that it has learned to seek, and finds a new child who is about to be born. It goes to this child and waits for the child to be born. With its first breath, the child breathes in this soul and it becomes someone new.

When someone experiences journeying, some part of them recognizes that they have done this before. With this, they begin to realize that they are more than the ego. This is a good beginning for their practice, as it weakens the usual resistance of the ego, which makes the rest of the process considerably easier.

I also recommend that the client commits to a daily practice, involving meditation/Soul Awareness, journeying and informal practice. The informal practice can be as simple as checking in to see how you are feeling; recognizing that whatever you are feeling is coming from ego and that ego has no substance of its own. Ego is only an interface between Soul and the body. This realization is often enough to trigger Soul Awareness. Once in Soul Awareness, simply rest in that expanded sense of luminous space. This part of you is one that will remain after the death of your body, and it knows that, so experiencing it reminds your whole Self that death is not an end for all of you.

With cases of approaching or imminent death, I encourage the client to clear up any obstacles to a good relationship with their ancestors and to journey to the Lower World to connect with them directly, as well as establishing an ancestor altar in their home. This relationship makes a huge difference in how the client experiences the passage through death.

When the client is actively in the process of dying, often no longer capable of conscious communication, I journey on their behalf to their ancestors to ask that they have someone present when they leave their body for the last time. I sometimes accompany their soul as well into the timeless space between the living world and the place of the ancestors. This space, which the Tibetans refer to as the Bardos, is dreamlike and often frightening. I have found that having a sense that you are not alone during this passage is very comforting.

Passage through the Bardos can take from a few days to a few months, depending on the circumstances of the death, state of awareness, and the relationship with ancestors. Once the soul arrives in the Lower World, the process is generally much more resolved and requires no input from the shaman.

This is necessarily a brief overview. The topic of what happens to us after death is much larger and more complex than could be addressed in this book. These teachings provide an overall structure for how the process works. Filling in the details takes direct experience.

Chapter 17

Spiritual Practice

Some teachings cannot be received by the physical brain.
– Grandfather

There are some realizations which cannot be received or processed with the physical brain alone. They require enough shen (the Qi we think with) to allow the transmission to be received. Much of the spiritual practice of post-tribal shamanism is about cultivating the necessary density of shen and using these realizations to further the process of awakening and integration of the whole Self.

Spiritual practice is a way of getting onto, and staying on, a path of spiritual awakening. What it is at the beginning is not what it is later on. Those first steps are important. They may even define the quality of your practice for many years to come. It is what you are doing in this moment, though, which is the key to your practice. Are you mindful of the thoughts, sensations, and emotions moving through you? Do you feel overly attached to these inner events, or are they flowing freely through you? Do you feel that you are the person thinking these thoughts, or does your sense of Self expand beyond this body and brain into the vast empty spaciousness within? It doesn't so much matter what the answers are to these questions, since they will change as you continue walking your path. What is important is that questions get asked and that change does happen.

Post-tribal shamanism is a pragmatic practice. If a technique doesn't work, why would anyone use it? If it does work, it must achieve something substantive in daily life, or it is not worth the time and energy we put into it. In my own life, these techniques have helped me to emerge from a hellish existence and into one which gives me daily bouts of joy and gratitude. This practice allows you to deal with adversity with deep calm, to recognize and receive the myriad blessing of Spirit, and to experience the naturally arising gifts of the soul.

In addition to its practical nature, post-tribal shamanism is always about the individual in relationship to community. In this sense community can mean anything from the ancestral soul, which contains the whole blood line of the family, to those people who are immediately impacted by your presence, to the whole of human communal consciousness. It is never just about 'you.' What you do to improve your life will affect everyone you are connected to, and that is your community.

Spiritual Practice refers to a dedicated, rigorous and regular use of spiritual techniques such as meditation, for spiritual purposes, such as awakening, realization, or connection with the divine. At the core of the shamanic spiritual practice is the synergy between Soul Awareness and ordinary consciousness. This leads to the gradual integration of the everyday consciousness into Soul Awareness.

Being dedicated means that you do the practice for a spiritual purpose. In this case, the purpose is to connect with, awaken, and eventually to integrate into, your own Soul Awareness.

Rigorous means that, when resistance arises, one practices anyway. When something gets in the way, causing a lapse in practice, one returns to the practice as soon as possible, rather than being defeated by the lapse.

Regular means daily. The best time to meditate is just after waking in the morning. Your mind is at its most receptive. Your body is rested and your spirit is most open. Waiting until evening is not as successful. However, meditating daily, no matter when, is essential to developing an effective spiritual practice.

If you do not already know how to meditate, it is a good idea to begin with the concentration exercise of single pointed internal focus. You simply choose one point, say your heart center, and focus your attention there, releasing all other thoughts, feelings, and sensations. The practice is honed by focusing into a smaller and smaller point. You may begin with a focal point the size of a golf ball, and proceed to one the size of a grain of rice, eventually working towards a single spark, like the point of a pin.

Ultimately, meditation is neither a formal, nor an informal practice. It is sitting and letting go of everything else. Awareness arises naturally, because it is our natural state. It is what we were born with. It is the state we rested in before we were born. It is what we return to when the mind quiets. It is only our resistance to letting go of the furious chatter of our lives that keeps us from that stillness.

You will begin to experience indications that your practice is working after the first few weeks or months. Some of these arise during the practice itself. You may find that you lose track of time, or that your body seems to disappear. Emerging from deep stillness, you may find it difficult to want to move, as if you were having trouble engaging your ordinary relationship with your physical body. You will probably come to enjoy the practice so much that you find it is difficult to return to ordinary consciousness. All of these are naturally arising symptoms of effective practice. Some or all of these will occur with regular sitting.

Beyond what happens during your sitting practice, other symptoms of effective practice will begin to arise in your everyday life, especially once you have begun working with Soul Awareness. These symptoms include an increased sense of equanimity, spontaneous moments of joy, with no apparent cause, and generally a more compassionate regard for yourself and others.

Much of this is due to the nature of the soul, or the part of the soul that has lived many lifetimes and is still intimately connected with the One. Experience has taught me – and countless others before me – that this soul does not generate fear, hatred or rage. It does provide bliss, joy and compassion, along with a profound sense of connection, well-being and communion.

We are all made up of many parts. This is true on a physical level and on a spiritual level as well. Just as our physical body is made up of heart, lungs, bones and blood, our spiritual self is composed of parts from the ancestors, parts that have lived before and parts that arise from this particular juxtaposition of these souls and this body in this time and place. The ancestral part of our soul is communal in nature. This means that it identifies as your whole bloodline, rather than with you as a separate individual. This can be confusing for those raised in our culture, where the individual is really all we experience as self.

The awakened shamanic practice teaches how to maintain awareness of both communal and individual self, and to use the synergy between both – between all these diverse parts – to enrich and benefit your practice.

The nature of these practices is non-material, and therefore it is difficult to put them into words that clearly relate to the direct experience. We use words like 'soul', 'awareness', 'awakening' – all of which refer to a real and profound experience, but which are difficult to define outside of that experience. Don't be concerned if the definitions leave you more confused than you were before. The important thing is the experience. Once you have that, the descriptions no longer matter, except as a means of communicating your experience to others.

When I speak of 'soul', I mean those parts of the Self which have neither a physical substance to them nor are dependent on the physical for their continuity. I refer to the intellectual awareness of the self, based in the experience derived through the physical senses as the ego.

I differentiate between consciousness and Awareness in that consciousness is a product of the embodied state, which makes necessary a subject/object relationship with the surrounding world. Awareness is the non-dual state of the soul, which does not differentiate between Self and Other.

We all come into this world in this state of Soul Awareness, not yet recognizing a separation between self and mother, but it gradually fades into the background as we develop ego to deal with the whole being in a body thing. The awareness of the ancestral soul is communal, and so it sees no real difference between you and anyone else in your bloodline. The awareness of your celestial soul is more universal. This is the part that exists beyond the confines of time and space. It is our connection with the great Mystery, however you may choose to express that.

Post-tribal shamanic practice is pragmatic. We deal with the spiritual, because it is there and not to deal with it would make our perception incomplete, and thus not be able to offer valid and effective results for everyday life.

Post-tribal shamanic spiritual practice is the means by which we bring the soul and the ego together into the ambiguous relationship that is the awakened self. It is a simple practice. You find your way to Soul Awareness and then you rest there, for at least 20 minutes a day, every day. You honor your ancestors on a regular basis and pay your respects to any other spirits that are in your vicinity, and when you have time, you continue to work on bringing all of these parts of yourself into greater and greater integration. Simple!

What happens when a person engages in this sort of practice is that the sense of self begins to shift away from the ego and toward a larger and more connected experience. More often than not, the ego responds to this shift with resistance, fear, anxiety, anger, and a whole range of tactics to derail the process. One of the ways to prove that you are more than your ego is to choose a path with which it is uncomfortable and stick to it, until the ego surrenders. With practice, ego becomes a willing participant and a powerful resource in the process of awakening.

If you walk the path of the shaman long enough, engaging in it as a spiritual practice, you will come to the experience of Soul Awareness, and to the further experience of being both soul and ego, simultaneously; of being able to juggle the dual and non-dual without dropping either one. This is accomplished by gradually integrating your thoughts, actions, feelings and form into Soul Awareness. This integration is achieved by remaining experientially connected in Soul Awareness, while your ego and body continue to operate in the world. It is a good idea to begin with simple physical movements and mindful observation of your thoughts. As you observe these movements and thoughts, they gradually dissolve into Soul Awareness. This dissolution brings these disparate elements into Soul Awareness, integrating them into the oneness of soul.

Another way to look at this process is that this spacious sense of luminous awareness already exists before you go looking for it. It was there before 'you' were born, before any of this world came into being. When the ego quiets down enough for us to observe this pre-existing condition it seems to us a great and marvelous discovery. This is often referred to as Awakening, but it is actually just a matter of being quiet enough to sense what was there before we started making such a fuss.

The process of integration is continuous. Even if you managed to integrate all that you are in this moment, there would be new elements arising in the next moment, and so on. There are so many pieces to the puzzles we think of as our selves, it is amazing that we manage, through the application of ego, to hold all of it together and function as individuals, rather than the communal representatives that we are.

The spiritual practice of post-tribal shamanism begins right where you are, in this very moment. Consider that the part of you which is conscious of your thoughts, sensations and feelings is a reflection of something much larger. See if you can, just for a moment, sense that Source which you are reflecting, and bask in that light.

Endnotes

i   As mentioned earlier, if the potential client exhibits signs that they are outside your scope of practice, you have a responsibility to pass them on to someone who can help them such as a reputable psychotherapist.

ii 'Karen' is a compilation of a few different cases, compiled to protect their identity.

iii These locations vary somewhat, depending on what map is being used. For instance, modern acupuncture often places the upper two burners in the solar plexus and heart center.

iv The tissue between the anus and genitals.

v   Carl Jung agrees.

Moon Books invites you to begin or deepen your encounter with Paganism, in all its rich, creative, flourishing forms.